D1094615

I DREAM OF
WOODY

I DREAM OF
WOODY

Dee Burton

William Morrow and Company, Inc.   New York 1984

Library of Congress Catalog Card Number: 83-63297

ISBN: 0-688-01556-5

Printed in the United States of America

First Edition

1 2 3 4 5 6 7 8 9 10

Book Design by Allan Mogel

ACKNOWLEDGMENTS

I thank:

Kristina Lindbergh, my editor, for her expertise, insight and thoughtfulness;

Meredith Bernstein, Lady Borton, Toby Kramer, James Landis, Myles Slatin and Bob Weide, for reading and commenting on parts of the manuscript for this book;

Frank Brady, for suggesting the book's title;

Pat Dubren, Ron Dubren, Harold Fuggian, Edith Grace Hodge, Mary Lyn Maiscott and Jo-Ann Monte, for reasons they will know;

and

most of all, the 112 "dreamers," for sharing with me their thoughts, feelings and dreams about Woody Allen.

—Dee Burton

CONTENTS

CONTENTS

INTRODUCTION

Deborah entered her subway station at about 10 A.M. She was late for work as usual. An hour earlier she'd have had to squeeze into a train jammed with commuters. But now the subway station was practically deserted. She opened a paperback novel and prepared to wait patiently for the next train.

As she stood reading Deborah noted that a man in a khaki raincoat had arrived at her platform. Out of habit she kept track of the man while continuing to focus on her novel.

The man began to walk directly toward her. She glanced across the track and saw that there was a commuter on the other side with her in clear view. That, combined with the fact that it was daytime, assured her she was safe. She relaxed. This was a familiar scenario. "Too familiar even to entertain me with a little healthy anxiety," she thought.

The man arrived at Deborah's side. She instinctively pulled the paperback novel closer to her face and bent her head down further. She stared at the book. All she could see from the corner of her eye was the raincoat again.

"Excuse me, miss. Would you like to go on a date right now?" the man said.

"What?"

"I said, excuse me, miss. Would you like to go on a date right now?"

There was an appealing quality to the man's voice. But Deborah was caught off guard—or rather, she was caught *on* guard—and once more her instinct for self-protection prevailed.

"No," she said, as she raised her eyes to see the terrified face of Woody Allen.

A dream from the collection? No. Not even a fantasy or a scene from an upcoming Woody Allen movie. The subway story is about the real-life Woody Allen. The incident was

9

related by Deborah Duanes, one of the women interviewed for this book. It was after her underground encounter with Allen that Deborah began to dream about him.

I Dream of Woody is about Woody Allen. However, rather than being the view of a film critic or a biographer, it is the collective view of some of the members of Woody Allen's audience. Its focus is on the appearance of the film-maker in the dreams of his fans, the effects of those appearances on the dreamers and what they indicate about the cultural significance of Allen's work.

Several of the men and women interviewed for this book had their first dreams about Allen after seeing him in person. But even for persons whose chance encounters prompted dreams, the content of their dreams reflects the personality and philosophy of Woody Allen as they have come to know him through his work. It is because of the poignancy and relevance of Allen's art—his films and stories—that he is projected into the dreams of his audience. The appearance of Allen in these dreams is an example of how deeply some men and women identify with the Woody Allen psyche.

Eighty dreams from seventy dreamers are included in this book. None of the dreams are daydreams or fantasies. All are dreams that occurred while the dreamers were asleep. And all of these dreams were reported in in-person interviews that followed an extensive screening procedure. The objective of *I Dream of Woody* is to provide a glimpse of the art, philosophy and personality of Woody Allen as experienced on both a conscious and an unconscious level by his fans.

Why Woody Allen? There exists no survey of the relative frequency with which various well-known figures appear in the dreams of their public. Nor is there any book, besides this one, that examines a collection of dreams about a particular person. Dreams are, after all, the most personal way in which someone we don't know can enter our lives—not only because we can interact intimately with the person as part of our often entertaining dream scenarios, but, more important, because our dreams originate from the deepest parts of our inner worlds. Considering this, it is remarkable that sets of dreams about famous people have never before been compiled.

There are a number of reasons why Woody Allen was the choice for this book—some of them purely personal. I myself have dreamed about Woody Allen, and, like many of the men and women I interviewed, I identify in many ways with the Woody Allen psyche. Of course, a person known through film or television seems more likely to appear in the dreams of his audience, because of the visual associations, than does someone known mainly through the print media. And among filmmakers and film and television personalities, Woody Allen is an especially logical choice as a dream object because he writes, directs and stars in most of his films and because his work seems to be significantly autobiographical. And, since there is a consistency in the characters Allen portrays in his films, the Allen persona is more likely to register and remain vivid in even the most casual moviegoer's memory.

Woody Allen's artistic sensibility also makes him an excellent choice as a dream object. Most of the underlying themes of his movies, stories, plays and earlier stand-up routines—mortality, sexuality, anxiety and the ongoing struggle to find meaning in a society that appears to value shallowness—are universal issues that affect people at the level of their unconscious. Woody Allen works directly from his inner world. The humor and the anxiety he depicts seem to spring consistently from his own unconscious. And so the likelihood of his entering into the unconscious of his audience may be greater than it would be for an actor-filmmaker whose work originated largely on a conscious level.

* * *

Woody Allen may well appear in the dreams of millions of people. And there are as many reasons why Allen might appear in a dream as there are people dreaming about him, since dreams usually reveal more about the dreamer than about the dream object. However, there are also patterns that emerge in dreams about a famous person, just as there are patterns of associations with other objects we dream about. It is thus that we are able to make generalizations about what that object symbolizes. And while an isolated symbol tells us less about a particular dreamer than would an idiosyncratic interpretation of his dream, it can sometimes help reveal the universal significance of the dream. Also, the context in which the symbolic object appears in a dream can reveal a great deal about the object itself.

I Dream of Woody focuses more on the dream object, Woody Allen, than on the dreamers. It addresses the question, what does Woody Allen symbolize for some of the members of his audience?

Who dreams about Woody Allen? With a very few exceptions, the dreamers are people who empathize intensely with Allen and usually also identify with him. This stands to reason because not only did these men and women dream about Allen, they responded to an ad, went through a telephone screening and took the time to come to an in-depth, in-person interview for which there was no remuneration.

To identify with another person means both to empathize and to feel an alikeness with that person. Needless to say, identification with famous people is common. The destructive effects of intense identification are well known. Replacing one's identity with that of another can severely limit one's psychological growth. However, identification can also have constructive effects. Constructive identification has three features: it enhances an individual's own identity rather than supplanting it with that of another; it operates to some degree on a conscious level—the individual is aware that he identifies with the public figure or other person; and it satisfies healthy needs, such as needs for achievement, risk taking and expansion, rather than self-limiting ones.

In interviewing the men and women for this book I was struck by the fact that many of them used their identification with Woody Allen to improve their lives—in a remarkable variety of ways. They harnessed it to conquer stage fright, to work through divorce, to stick out a doctoral dissertation, to resolve a theological conflict, and to overcome depression. Clearly, not all of the people interviewed identify with Allen in constructive ways. But the majority of the dreamers perceive the filmmaker as being like themselves—and in positive ways. They feel like Allen's peers, not often in artistic achievement, but almost always in artistic aspirations and in terms of a shared outlook on life.

The dream lives of these men and women parallel and sometimes transcend their waking-life identification with Allen. In some of the dreams the dreamer learns something directly from Allen—attains an insight—that remains with him after he awakens, and helps him to make a meaningful change in his life. In others Allen comforts the dreamer, usually by helping him to feel protected or to know he is not alone in his feelings. But whether posing as a basketball player, a graduate adviser or a lover, Woody Allen as dream object frequently helps his dreamer. However, there is a darker theme that cuts across many of the dreams—one of disillusionment. Some of the men and women admitted that the dreams in which Allen disappointed them reflect their conscious perceptions of the artist. Other dreamers were startled by the new insights these dreams brought them.

I'd have liked to interview dreamers in Red Cloud, Nebraska, or in Vienna, Tokyo or Paris, but practical considerations of time and money made it necessary to limit the study geographically. New York was the obvious choice for the primary interview site, since it is Allen's favorite city, to which he paid homage with the visually stunning film *Manhattan*. And as a compliment, Allen's least favorite city, Los Angeles, was chosen as the second interview site. This bicoastal choice does not in any way stem from considerations about Allen's popularity in Middle America or elsewhere. The universality of Woody Allen's work is well established. In fact, when early word leaked out about this project, I was inundated with phone calls and letters from Japan, Italy, Germany, Austria, Belgium, Canada and all across the United States.

Dreamers were recruited primarily through ads placed in newspapers in the two cities. Telephone interviews constituted the second step of the screening. The objectives of the call were to screen out men and women who had fantasies rather than dreams to offer and those who would in any way be questionable subjects, including, for example, one very articulate gentleman who volunteered to dress up like Woody Allen and come over to my place. If I had no reason to think that the respondent was fabricating a dream or mistaking a fantasy for a dream, I scheduled an in-person interview. Why did 112 men and women go out of their way to respond to a newspaper ad, answer questions over the telephone and submit to in-person interviews that lasted between forty-five minutes and five hours, without any tangible compensation for their trouble? For the same reason, I think, that they dreamed about Allen: because Woody Allen is important to them. For these men and women an opportunity to share their feelings about the filmmaker with an interested investigator was apparently a reward in itself.

Each interview began with questions about personal data. I then asked each subject several questions about Woody Allen: whether he had ever met or seen Allen, whether he'd seen all of Allen's movies, his favorite Woody

Allen film, his waking-life opinion of Allen, how many dreams he'd had about him and the approximate dates of those dreams.

Next I asked the subject to tell me his dream or dreams. When he had finished relating a dream we discussed it in detail: whether it was in color, what the dreamer felt like, what Woody was wearing, whether there were other people in the dream, what Woody felt for the dreamer, whether the dreamer felt any differently about Woody Allen after having the dream, how often he remembers dreams and so forth.

The interview then became completely open. Some of the dreamers had already given great consideration to the significance of their dreams; some kept regular dream journals; a couple of dreamers had discussed their Woody dreams in therapy; a few had written down their dreams about Woody even though they don't usually do so, because the dreams were exceptional in some way.

From a total of 144 dreams that were told to me by 112 final subjects, I chose eighty dreams of seventy men and women to include in *I Dream of Woody*. These I selected mainly on the bases of whether they represented recurring themes and/or whether they were interesting to read. An occasional dream is included because there is something striking about the dreamer, though the dream itself is not remarkable. If one were to read the dreams not included in this book, he would find that the themes represented are similar to those of the dreams in the book, but that the excluded dreams have fewer details, less concrete imagery and less novelty.

The seventy subjects whose dreams are reported consist of thirty-nine women (56 percent) and 31 men (44 percent). They range in age from nineteen years to fifty-nine years, the median age being twenty-nine years. Fifteen of the dreamers are from Los Angeles and fifty-five are from New York.

Forty-four percent of the dreamers are Jewish, 29 percent are Protestant, 21 percent are Catholic and 6 percent had other religious backgrounds. It's interesting to note that of the total, only 12 percent of the men, compared to 40 percent of the women had had Protestant upbringings, but 56 percent of the men and 35 percent of the women had had Jewish upbringings. This in itself may reflect an attitude toward the Jewish boy–WASP girl coupling featured in so many Woody Allen movies. Forty percent of the dreamers work in the creative or performing arts, and 18 percent of the dreamers are therapists, counselors or social scientists. The others had a wide variety of occupations.

Three fourths of the dreamers have seen all but one or two of Woody Allen's movies. Overall, the favorite film is *Annie Hall,* with *Manhattan* a close second. Surprisingly, one half of the men and women have seen Woody Allen in person, usually just once (and most at Michael's Pub, where Allen has, for years, been playing the clarinet in a New Orleans jazz band on Monday nights). Eight of the dreamers who have seen Allen in the flesh have also met him, and three of them have worked briefly with the filmmaker.

Again, the participants in this study are not just casual observers of Allen's work. They are Woody Allen fans. The researcher does not attempt to tell what a typical moviegoer thinks of Woody Allen. Rather, I set out to reveal what it is about Allen that deeply affects some people—what he symbolizes for his fans. The information that follows should not be viewed as data from a random sampling of subjects in a scientific survey, but as data from case studies of Woody Allen enthusiasts.

While the eighty dreams have eighty different plots, there are themes that are repeated throughout the set of dreams. Several of these themes have been used to organize the dreams. Certainly, most of the dreams have more than one theme and are therefore relevant to more than one section.

Each dream is introduced with a description of the dreamer. All names of dreamers are fictitious, with the exception of the first name of the first dreamer, Fred (the reason for this exception will be apparent on reading the dream). Personal data have been modified for a few of the dreamers in order to ensure their anonymity. Otherwise, all data are real.

Death is the big obsession behind all the things I've done.

—Woody Allen

If you want to find a good tip, find a good rabbi.

—Dream Woody

Death is the big obsession behind all the
things I've done.
—Woody Allen

If you want to make God laugh, tell him about your
plans.
—Diane Woody

THE
DREAM
MAN

Quirky Woody

The Woody Allen of fans' dreams often behaves in a peculiar way, offers odd explanations for his behavior or sets up events to appear to be what they are not. Dreams about Allen often have surprise endings, reflecting not just the unpredictability common to dreams but the perverseness of Allen's personality as projected by the dreamers.

•

FRED FORMAN is a twenty-four-year-old native New Yorker who is just beginning his career as a composer. Fred used to feel sorry for Allen on the basis of the Woody persona of the filmmaker's early movies. Consider, for instance, Virgil Starkwell, in *Take the Money and Run* (1969), whose bank-robbery attempt was foiled by his bad handwriting. "I've got a gub," the bank teller read from Virgil's holdup note. "What's a gub?" the teller wanted to know. And Virgil's clever attempt to escape from prison by carving a fake gun out of a bar of soap failed when it began to rain, causing the make-believe gun to dissolve in his hands. And there was *Bananas'* (1971) Fielding Mellish who, even after becoming a revolutionary and a world leader in an attempt to please his woman (played by Louise Lasser), still leaves her feeling that, romantically, "something's missing." And Allan Felix in *Play It Again, Sam* (play, 1969; film, 1972) found his enormous anxiety over women reinforced by the repeated rejections he received: "Beat it, creep!" was the subtle rebuff of one woman Allan politely asked to dance. But after seeing *Manhattan* (1979), portraying the professionally successful and sexually attractive Isaac Davis, Fred decided that Allen really has a good life after all. Fred sees similarities in experiences he and Allen have had, especially those involving relationships with women. He also identifies with the sensitivity that, he thinks, comes from his and Allen's Jewish upbringing. Fred spotted Allen in person once: on Fifth Avenue, in 1974. He had the following dream during a visit to Paris in 1977.

MY BUDDY WOODY

A good friend and I were sitting on metal Samsonite chairs in a semicircle with several other people whom I did not know but who were also sitting on metal Samsonite chairs. There were pillars in the room which kept me from seeing the other people. But I could see my friend Jon seated next to me.

The door to the room opened and in walked Woody Allen. He walked right over to me, without hesitating, and said, "Hello, Fred." I was thrilled! I felt a real rush. "Hi, Woody," I said.

But then Woody walked up to my friend Jon and said, "Hello, Fred," to him, too! And Allen then proceeded to greet each person in the room by the name of Fred.

I was bewildered. When Woody had finished with his greetings, I walked up to him. "Why did you call everyone by my name!" I demanded of him.

"Your name?" Woody asked, puzzled at first. And then, "Oh, no," he explained. "Fred is just a name I use for people I don't know."

Fred's funny-sad dream seems to be about alienation: People sitting on stiff Samsonite chairs in a room with pillars that prevent Fred from seeing anyone except his friend Jon, the one person he feels a connection to. Then Dream Woody enters and, at first, appears to serve the function he does for many fans: he takes away their sense of alienation. But in this case, the connection between Woody and the dreamer turns out to be illusory.

According to Fred, his dream confirmed that because Woody Allen is a celebrity, he is inaccessible to him. "I was just anonymous and he reduced me." Fred's feelings about Allen have changed since the dream. "I'd still like to talk to him about writing, but I don't want to give him any praise. And I'd prefer not to dream about him again."

Fred's dream is the only one of the collection in which the dreamer feels Allen is inaccessible by virtue of his celebrityhood. Remarkably, almost half of the dreamers expect that they will one day get to know—not just meet—Woody Allen. However, Fred's dream does echo a quality that Dream Woody manifests in several other dreams, namely, that he giveth and he taketh away.

•

PAT EPSTEIN is an actress who wants to work with Woody Allen. "And I take myself seriously enough as an actress to say that without laughing." According to Pat, her passion for life is tied up with her passion for wanting to work with Allen. Whenever she feels enthusiastic and motivated, it's usually because of some thought about the filmmaker. Pat used to have extreme stage fright but "learned from Woody that the point of life is to share and not be scared." Like Allen, she loves New York even though it creates in her "a need to scream and cry." She remembers dreams almost every day, and had the following dream on April 5, 1980.

WITH FEATHERS

Through a connection, I finally got a chance to audition for a Woody Allen film—for the part of a character who has a pet bird. I was told ahead of time that part of my audition would involve playing with a bird. This was awful luck because I have a terrible phobia about birds—something to do with wings! But I wanted this part so badly that I was willing to give it my best try.

I arrived for the audition and entered into a small room. Woody Allen was seated, and he was holding a tiny bird in his hand. I tried to convince myself that the bird was cute.

Woody described the part in detail. But all the while I was staring at the bird, trying to psych myself up. "It's just a cute little bird," I kept repeating to myself.

Woody then extended his hand. Bravely I took the bird. The bird immediately took off, flapping his wings, flying around my head, landing on my hand, and then taking off again. His wings fluttered at an amazing speed. I was proud of my bravery.

Woody handed me a script, and we went through the lines together. Woody was not at all warm. He was very businesslike. He did get nicer when he noticed how nervous I was. But he was just a little too nice then—the way people get when they're sure they don't want you.

We finished reading the script, and Woody left the room in silence. I sat down in this small cubicle of a room to wait. Surprisingly quickly, Woody stepped back into the room. "By the way," he said. "If you get the part, that bird is not the bird you'll be working with."

Then he stepped out of the room once more for just a second. He was back in a flash to finish his point. "This," he said, "is the real bird." Clinging to his shoulder was an eagle.

Remembering Sandy Bates's reaction to a pigeon who flew into his apartment (in *Stardust Memories*), it's hard to picture Woody Allen interacting so calmly with birds. "They're—they're—they're rats with wings," he said, flinging magazines at the bird. ". . . get it out of here. It's probably one of those killer pigeons."

Pat obviously responds well to a challenge. She woke up from her dream feeling more motivated than ever to work with Woody Allen. The dream is a reminder of how Pat, in her waking life, overcame stage fright by thinking of Allen, and it suggests she is ready for greater challenges.

"Intelligence is the swiftest of birds," according to the *Rig-Veda*. And the tiny bird with which Dream Woody initially challenged Pat had wings that "fluttered at an amazing speed." Having met this challenge bravely, Pat was then presented with the loftier ambitions symbolized by the eagle. On one level, Pat's dream can be seen as symbolizing a challenge to her intellect. On another level, the dream shows a struggle to activate her spirituality. Birds in mythology most often represent the way to immortality: birds symbolize the soul, and birds in flight, the soul's ascension into heaven. The eagle then can be seen as representing the ultimate step in this ascension, or in the struggle to transcend the material world. As a group, Woody Allen's fans see him as someone who is continually probing his unconscious and struggling to come to terms with issues that go beyond the material concerns of contemporary society. And the symbolism in many of their dreams, like Pat's, reflects identification with these issues.

•

DAVE BRECK is a copy editor for a magazine. He identifies with Allen's vulnerability and with his dislike for pseudointellectuals. And he suspects that his affinity for Allen is intensified by the fact that the filmmaker resembles a childhood friend. Dave had the following dream not long after seeing *Stardust Memories* in 1980.

——————————————— **THE RECLUSE** ———————————————

Woody and I had been friends for some time. We both enjoyed the friendship. We felt comfortable with each other and we had a lot of interests in common.

Woody had a new film out at this time and he was eager to know what people really thought of it. He wanted to go to a neighborhood theater where his new film was playing and where no one knew he would be present, in order to observe the spontaneous reactions of a typical audience. I agreed to this.

Woody kept stressing how important it was that no one see him. He said that we should wait until a couple of minutes after the houselights were down and then quickly sneak into the back row of the theater.

I assured Woody that I would be careful, but he kept repeating those instructions. He was very concerned that someone might recognize him. "We have to be very quiet," he told me. Fortunately, we were successful. Shortly after the houselights went down, we entered the theater. The theater was about two thirds full, but luckily there were two seats in the back row. We took the seats and began to watch the movie.

We had been there only about ten minutes or so when Woody got up and moved up a couple of rows. I didn't know why he had moved, but I continued to watch the movie. In a few more minutes, however, Woody again got up and moved up to another seat. I began to get quite nervous; I thought someone was bound to notice him if he kept changing seats. But, indeed, Woody did change seats again—and then again! Finally, Woody rose and walked all the way down the aisle to the front of the theater and walked across in front of the movie screen. At this point, the whole audience saw and recognized him!

Woody started walking up the other aisle and now all of his fans rose from their seats and started chasing and yelling after him. As he came running up the aisle toward the door—his fans in hot pursuit—Woody turned and shouted to me on his way out: "You see what I mean? I can't go anywhere without this happening!"

Dave's dream was a turning point in his appreciation of Woody Allen. Before the dream, Allen was the person Dave most wanted to meet. But Dave thinks his dream gave him "intuition into Allen's real self" and that the filmmaker is really a hypocrite. Dave says he expects to continue to admire Allen's work, but that his affection for him is gone.

It is striking that the disillusionment dreams of several of the dreamers are so strong that they alter the dreamer's conscious perceptions of Allen. In Dave's case, his dream seems to be a response to *Stardust Memories,* in which Allen plays Sandy Bates, a famous film director who feels victimized by his fans, depicted in the movie as self-centered, pushy people. Bates, like the real-life Allen, travels in his own chauffeur-driven Rolls-Royce. By "hypocritical," Dave means that while Allen presents himself in interviews as someone with meaningful values who, for instance, doesn't think money is important, he may actually be living a materialistic, self-serving life-style.

●

ALICE BARTHE is a twenty-year-old college student who enjoys writing poetry. She grew up on Long Island in an atheistic household. She likes mice a lot and raised them as a child. Alice had her "first major relationship" recently on a three-month visit to California and says that at the time she identified with the experiences of both the Woody Allen and Diane Keaton characters (Alvy and Annie) in *Annie Hall:* with their conflicts and struggles to make their relationship work. At the time of the interview Alice had had three dreams about Woody Allen. The following, her first, is from February 17, 1975.

THE MOUSE-BABY

I arrived at the fountain in Central Park. A crowd had gathered around the fountain. I moved closer to see what they were watching.

The crowd drawers turned out to be two mouse-babies swimming around in freezing cold water. The babies had the bodies of human infants, but their facial features were mouselike and they had tails. I saw that one mouse-baby had been cut in half.

Woody Allen approached the fountain and called out to the crowd. "The mouse or baby is illegitimate!" he announced. "Still, it's my own mouse or baby! The mother was a beautiful girl from the revolution. Unfortunately, she died at childbirth."

I turned back to the fountain and discovered that the mouse-baby who had been cut in half had died. At this point I dashed to the fountain to save the remaining mouse-baby.

I took the mouse-baby to my apartment and put him to bed. Then I sat down to watch TV. There was a knock on the door.

I opened the door to two irate black girls. They told me that I had taken the mouse-baby out of his normal environment, and they threatened to kill me if I didn't give the mouse-baby back. I asked them to please sit down, and I tried to reason with them.

There was another knock. I again opened the door, this time to a huge black woman wearing a yellow shawl and carrying a baby in her arms. "I'm the babysitter," she said.

"We have no baby," I said emphatically.

"Well, make believe you have a baby," she retorted. And she walked right in and sat down in front of the TV.

I had barely sat back down when some middle-aged men entered. One of the men apparently was my husband. And he came through the door already talking about how bad I am because I won't let him and his friends in the living room.

My husband and the other men left almost immediately. And

even as they walked up the street I could hear them talking about sex and getting old. When I next became aware of what was happening I was walking up a never-ending hallway. This infinite corridor was narrow and dark. I could see only that it was painted blue. As I walked endlessly up this hallway, I could hear people repeating my last name with different accents: "Barthe," "Barthe," "Barthe. . . ."

The montagelike quality of this dream, which might be seen as representing various stages of life—birth (of the mouse-babies, resulting in their mother's death), aging (Alice's middle-aged husband and their friends discussing growing old), escaping from death (of the mouse-baby Alice saves), threat of death (to Alice by the two black girls) and death itself (the mouse-babies' mother and one mouse-baby)—suggests the experience of life rushing before one's eyes as one recognizes the inevitability of one's death. The dreamer's awareness of mortality is reinforced by symbols of contact with the unconscious: the fountain, the narrow, dark and never-ending hallway. And if the "beautiful girl from the revolution" is Alice, then the dream also represents rebirth after death. The continuity of all life is further emphasized by the interspecies babies and by the different accents with which people repeat Alice's last name. It is a striking dream for a girl approaching womanhood (Alice was sixteen years old). Woody Allen's cameo appearance provides information on the background of the hybrid infants, but his role in the dream seems peripheral to the main themes. Alice says that while Allen's attitude in her dream was serious, he was really just making a joke about the situation.

Why was there a need for a stand-up comic routine in such a significant dream? Alice has described herself as someone with an active social life who is still lonely. And she says that Woody Allen sometimes assuages her loneliness. So perhaps Allen's role in this dream is exactly the one he plays in Alice's waking life: he is not directly involved with the matters of her life, but his presence reassures her. Thus, when Alice looks at a projected montage of her life, there has to be a scene for Woody Allen. Then, too, death is an obsession of Woody Allen's, so that his appearance in Alice's dream can also be seen as a symbol reinforcing the main themes: life stages and confronting death.

Artistic Integrity

Artistic integrity is a common theme of the dreams, and it is by far the most frequent attribute credited to Woody Allen in response to the question: "In your waking life, what do you think of Woody Allen?" Below are representative replies:

"He has the courage to carry his own individuality where it needs to go."
"As an artist, he expresses honest feelings."
"He perseveres."
"He's a maverick and a very strong person."
"He's a genius and he hasn't sold out."
"He faces his own personal weaknesses."
"He's America's most brilliant and honest filmmaker."

Risk taking is an important part of the artistic integrity that Allen's fans admire. He has taken significant risks throughout his career. He is a shy man. In her book . . . *But We Need the Eggs* (St. Martin's Press, 1982), Diane Jacobs observes that Allen "makes a virtue of his innate shyness." Nonetheless, shyness makes a lot of things difficult. In his interview of over twenty years ago with William Zinsser (*Saturday Evening Post,* September 21, 1963), Allen said that in the first grade he wanted to be a comedian but gave up the idea immediately because of stage fright. "The emotional terror of getting up in front of people has always been gigantic," he said. And so stepping out in 1962 for his debut at the

Duplex in Greenwich Village and performing his own stand-up material—the humor that he had for years been writing for other comics (including Sid Caesar and Bob Hope)—was very difficult for Allen. "I never worked on timing and delivery because those are natural," he said in his interview with Jacobs. "But I was scared, and I worked at feeling more at ease and getting to enjoy my time on stage." Risking failure as a performer early in his career was perhaps what made all the difference. How deprived we would be had Allen remained behind the scenes!

Allen's humorless *Interiors*, about the narcissistic, alienated but talented members of a family who feed self-destructively upon one another, and his brazenly contemptuous *Stardust Memories* were also clearly risks, the latter being one that failed to succeed either commercially or critically (*Stardust* is certainly a film that future audiences will look back on with greater affection than today's audience feels for it).

In an interview for Harold Mantell's 1977 film documentary *Woody Allen: An American Comedy*, published in *Media and Methods* (December 1977), Allen talked about risk taking and failing:

What's important to an artist is that he fails a certain amount of times. Whenever you look at great artists they have an enormous amount of failures as well as successes, whereas nonartists get into that terrible trap where they are constantly not risking because they want to have hits all the time—hit films, hit plays. They find a formula. . . . Chaplin's a guy whose instincts were correct—he was constantly trying to grow and failing. . . . If Chaplin did a film today, you'd still be interested in it. You'd still want to see what's on his mind because he was willing to fail.

Allen's words certainly apply to his own work. *Stardust Memories* stimulated curiosity as well as anger among the filmmaker's followers. Was this film a turning point in Allen's career? Did it mark the death of the Woody persona? Was it breaking ground for a new Allen genre? Was it just an aberration?

A Midsummer Night's Sex Comedy, about three turn-of-the-century couples on vacation together, provided a hint that the Woody persona might be growing: opening up emotionally (Andrew even told his wife "I hate you," when he learned that she'd been unfaithful to him—a direct expression of anger over being betrayed, of which Isaac Davis in *Manhattan* was not capable). It also showed more confidence in Allen's belief in the importance of living fully every moment and explored, however cautiously, the potential for optimistic spiritual ways of relating to death. However, with the exception of the main theme, "seize the moment," the attitudes in *A Midsummer Night's Sex Comedy* are expressed tentatively. There is little passion in the film. It's charming but not convincing, and perhaps was not intended to be so. Allen was open to exploring in this lighthearted interlude. And in so doing, he took the chance of ending up, as he did, with a film that is somewhat hollow. On the other hand, *Zelig*, about a first-generation American in the 1920s and '30s who was so desperate to fit in with other people that he developed a disorder in which he acquired the physical characteristics of whomever he was with, is the most technically experimental of all of Allen's films. "Every frame was a nightmare," said the film's coproducer, Jack Rollins, discussing the amount of work it required. But the work and the experimentation were rewarded with considerable critical acclaim. "*Zelig*," wrote Vincent Canby in *The New York Times* (July 15, 1983), "is Woody Allen's triumph. It's one more demonstration that he, rather than any of his more conventional, mainstream contemporaries, is the premier American film maker of his day."

The creation of the original Woody Allen film persona

was in itself a unique example of risk taking. From *Take the Money and Run* on, the character played by Allen on screen has projected his own emotions and attitudes with an honesty and detail that encourage his audience to believe they are seeing the real Woody Allen. At the same time, Allen, particularly in his pre-*Annie Hall* films, magnified his anxieties and fears and added derogatory characteristics that do not reflect his real-life attributes—such as clumsiness. Thus he created the schlep persona—the inept, cowardly loser—that many members of his audience came to assume was the real Woody Allen. (It is striking that not one of the men or women interviewed for this book described Woody Allen in terms of the early schlep persona.) Permitting himself to become identified as an unattractive, awkward schlemiel was a risk to his career and, perhaps, to his self-esteem. But the risk was rewarded instead by international fame for the Woody Allen persona.

However, as Allen's post-*Love and Death* films have become increasingly realistic, the Allen persona has likewise seemed to correspond even more closely to real-life Allen. In fact, in his 1974 interview with Leonard Probst at the New School for Social Research in New York, Allen was quite open about his intention to make his films increasingly realistic and personal. "Eventually," he said, "I would just like to come out and be myself." In some ways that is precisely what Allen has done, at least up to and including *Stardust Memories*. The false traits—such as athletic incompetence and insecurity with women—have melted away, the anxieties are less blown up, and the physical image of Woody Allen on screen is no longer shaped by the eye of his worst enemy.

This trend also constitutes a new risk for Allen, as it appears to yield new information about the man. The possibility that he might feel contempt for his fans was suggested by *Stardust Memories,* for instance, the first movie in which he played a character who does not elicit from his audience the warm feelings that the Allen schlep characters of *Bananas* and *Sleeper* did.

Intriguingly, as his films have become more and more self-revelatory, in interviews Allen has become increasingly insistent about denying that his work is autobiographical. This apparent turnabout could be a formula Allen has settled on to protect himself from the born-again nakedness of his work, or it may represent his frustration at being misinterpreted. In most of his films Allen presents his own obsessions so intensely that viewers have an unmistakable sense of contact with the real man, even though the facts of the movies may not represent his life.

•

ALMA VESLEY is an assistant advertising director for a well-known cosmetics company. Alma, who grew up in Wisconsin and now lives in Manhattan, loves New York for its proximity to so many beautiful beaches and would like to "let the waves at Amagansett pound me to a pulp." She says that *Annie Hall* makes "the ultimate statement about California." Alma thinks Allen's films, with the exception of *Interiors*, constitute the work of a genius. She's seen Woody Allen in real life once, at the Carnegie Deli on Seventh Avenue in Manhattan. Her dream is from February 1978.

_____ **ARTISTIC RISK** _____

Brooklyn is someplace I almost never go. Yet here I was walking along a quiet brownstone-lined Brooklyn street. A big crowd had gathered a block ahead of me and I hurried there to see what was happening.

A man pointed up to the fourth floor of a brownstone. There was Woody Allen, hanging an old black-and-white striped mattress—the kind you couldn't give away to the Salvation Army—out a window. Only he wasn't just hanging the mattress out of the window. Instead he was propping it in the window so that part of the mattress was wedged in and most of it was hanging out.

Woody intended to slide down the mattress and then take a headlong dive to see what would happen when he hit the pavement four floors below. It was an artistic happening.

The crowd was buzzing. "He's a genius. He must know what he's doing!" one man said.

"It certainly will be interesting because whatever he does is worth seeing," a woman commented.

A fire engine pulled up. Woody could kill himself with that jump. We all were concerned. But we understood that it didn't matter to Woody whether he lived or died. He was determined to do something different.

"He's given us so much," I thought. "If this is what he wants to do, who are we to stop him?"

The mattress was wedged in place. Woody leaned out of the window, ready for his descent.

A few months after her dream Alma saw *Interiors* and she now considers the dream to be her *Interiors* premonition dream. Although many of Allen's followers would disagree with Alma, she considers that movie to be an artistic failure. Like most of the dreamers, Alma felt closer to Woody Allen after dreaming about him. She doesn't think real-life Woody is as fatalistic as her Dream Woody, but that he is definitely as risk taking.

•

SCOTT GUNN is an admittedly homophobic Manhattan psychiatrist who says he would like to have Woody Allen as a patient. Scott says he identifies with Allen. That the way Allen (in his early movies) "glorified being clumsy and awkward and nerdy has made me much less uncomfortable about my own clumsy neurotic Jewish nerdiness." Scott also shares the top three interests Allen, as Isaac in *Manhattan*, dictated into his tape recorder as reasons for living: Groucho Marx, Willie Mays and the second movement of the Jupiter Symphony (Scott says classical music in general). Scott's favorite Allen movie is *Bananas*. The dream below, from early December 1979, is the second of three dreams he's had about Allen.

_____ **FOR ART'S SAKE** _____

I was observing the filming of a scene from a Woody Allen movie. It was a homosexual scene. Woody Allen was getting into bed with another man and both of them were nude.

I watched, astonished, as the two men began caressing. "My God," I thought, "there's nothing that man won't do for art!"

Scott says he had been aware of, and uncomfortable about, having "homosexual kinds of impulses . . . things like salivating or feeling my eyes widen, when I see or hear about an attractive man." But Woody Allen in Scott's dream was comfortable with playing a homosexual role in a movie, and that left Scott feeling more comfortable about his own homosexual feelings. Scott was also obviously impressed with Dream Woody's commitment to his art.

•

MAX BERNSTEIN is a financial adviser for public television. He respects Allen for "taking himself seriously and thereby creating a serious life in an absurd world." Max feels Allen used to be an existentialist but is now a Buddhist, *Manhattan* being the turning point in Allen's transition from one to the other—a transition Max is struggling to achieve in his own life. According to Max, Allen kept trying and working hard, and finally with *Manhattan* he experienced emotional freedom: he replaced the alienation of existentialism with the wisdom of Buddhism.

Max has seen Allen twice in real life, once on a Manhattan street and another time on an off-season ferry to Fire Island. On the latter occasion, Allen and Diane Keaton took seats in front of Max on an otherwise empty ferry. Max was concerned that his presence might inhibit their conversation, so he sensitively decided to move to the upper deck. In the process, however, Max turned into a Woody Allen character. Trying to slip away unobtrusively, Max tripped, slid across the floor and dumped a cup of coffee inches from the couple. The dream below is from April 30, 1979.

_____ **CABLE CARS** _____

Amy Irving's mother called me. "You stole something from my house!" she said. "Two people have told me so." I knew for a fact that one of the two was only eight years old.

It was an unpleasant incident. But I left my apartment determined to forget it. I took a subway to a stop near the Harlem River Bridge.

I exited the subway and aboveground was joined by Woody Allen. We walked through the streets of this poor neighborhood on our way to the bridge.

At the bridge I was confronted with cable cars. I was honestly afraid to strap myself into one of these and ride across high above the bridge and the water. Woody, however, just casually stepped into a car.

It was also intended that I hook my dog into a separate car for the ride. And I was frightened for my dog as well.

"I'll just walk," I said.

"There's an open place; you can't just walk across!" Woody told me.

"Then I'll get the car and meet you on the other side," I volunteered.

Woody threw me the car keys. I walked away in search of the automobile.

Suddenly my dog pulled on the leash. I looked up in time to see a Puerto Rican kid stealing a bike. I found a cop, and then my dog and I went with him to retrieve the bike. I was regaining my confidence.

As we stood with the kid and the bike, I glanced back in the direction of the bridge. I saw a woman who looked very much like a deceased friend of mine. And she was hooking her dog into a cable car to go across the Harlem River Bridge. The woman looked afraid, as I had been. And the Puerto Rican kid, as though guessing my thoughts, spoke up: "We lose about one dog a week that way."

I stared at the bridge with the cable cars silently vanishing above. I realized that Allen was probably on the other side of the bridge by now. I felt a real sense of admiration and respect for him for going out there ahead of me.

Max says that this ominous dream has helped him in his struggles to find emotional freedom, which for him means taking himself seriously, as Woody Allen does. The dream reinforced his commitment to "keep working and working and stay with where I think my center is." And it reminded him that "there are only a few peak experiences in life."

The bridge over the Harlem River might be seen as symbolizing the transition Max feels Allen has made from existentialism to Buddhism, the move that Max, in his dream, still fears. The dream reveals not just Max's fear for himself but his protective concern for his dog as well. Dream Woody's risk, being only for himself, was less than the one Max or the woman with her dog had to take. It could be the dream is suggesting that the philosophical growth Max pursues will be a more complex undertaking or require more effort from him than it did from Woody.

* * *

Several of the dreams illustrate an obsession on the part of the dreamer with trying to "catch up" with Woody Allen. Sometimes the obsession represents a wish to be literally with Allen (most often seen in women's dreams) and sometimes a desire to attain Allen's standards for art and/or morality (seen in both men's and women's dreams).

•

JASON WEIL is a twenty-six-year-old counselor who works with juvenile delinquents in Los Angeles. Woody Allen has been Jason's idol for years, to the extent that Jason used to dress like Woody, do comic monologues like him and "knew every line from every movie." He respects Allen for the emphasis Allen places on morals and integrity. Jason also feels an affinity for the filmmaker because they have had similar relationships with women. Not surprisingly, Jason has had many dreams about Woody Allen. And in some of these dreams the distinction between himself and Allen is blurred. The following dream, his first, is from 1970, when Jason was still in high school.

_____ A MAZE _____

I was in Beverly Hills with a friend, and we were crossing at a crosswalk. I thought I saw Woody Allen, but couldn't believe it. I nudged my buddy. ''Wasn't that Woody Allen?'' I said.

''Yeah,'' he answered with no enthusiasm.

''Well, why didn't you tell me? I want to go up to him.''

''He's a really private person,'' he reminded me. I knew he was right. So I let it go. ''I love the man so much I've got to respect his wishes,'' I thought of Woody.

That lasted about ten seconds. Then I turned and started after Woody.

Woody had crossed and was on the other side of the street

by now, but he was still within my sight. I tried to follow him, but the streets became an impossible maze. And then I knew I would never catch up with him. I continued, nonetheless, to try to make my way through the maze.

Mazes in dreams often represent intense longing on the part of the dreamer: they symbolize missed connections and loneliness. Jason felt even closer to Woody Allen after this dream, and says, "It strengthened in my mind my respect for him." The dream is, in one regard, an especially constructive one in that while Jason realizes he will not catch up with his idol, he still perseveres in pursuing the ideals Allen represents for him.

Jason doesn't think his identification with Allen—even though it is clearly worship—is destructive. He has quit dressing like Allen and imitating his life-style, and has chosen a very different career from the filmmaker's. But the affinity is still there, and growing stronger all the time, giving Jason a sense of the possibility of transcending his own limitations.

•

STEPHEN WOHL is a twenty-two-year-old film producer from L.A. who "grew up on Woody Allen." Stephen was in junior high school when he first became aware that he and Allen shared a great deal. "Here's someone who thinks like I do," he said to himself. He was cheered by this discovery of someone who shared his world view, because not many of his fellow twelve-year-olds felt either his anxiety about mortality and decaying morality on the one hand, or his artistic discipline on the other (Stephen wrote and directed his first film while he was still in junior high school). The following dream, which occurred toward the end of 1977, is representative of the many dreams Stephen has had about Allen.

_____ **THE CHASE** _____

I was watching a television program in which Woody Allen and Diane Keaton were walking together down a New York street. It was a point-of-view shot, which is a film term meaning that the camera takes the point of view of one of the characters. The point of view was that of someone following them, walking behind them. As I watched my TV, I wished it were me there walking behind them, following them. If I were there behind them, I imagined I would go up to them and start a conversation.

Suddenly: there I was on the street that had been on television. It was no longer a television program, but real life. And I was walking right behind Woody Allen and Diane Keaton and I really wanted to approach them and say something to them. But I experienced this problem that I also have in real life whenever I meet someone who's been very important to me. Namely, I didn't know what to say. I didn't want to say, "Your films have been very important to me," because that sounds corny. Fortunately, though, I did think of something to say to Woody that would be appropriate, that would let him know the thought was sincere without sounding too tacky.

I was at an intersection where Woody and Diane had just crossed the street. And something happened that used to happen to me in my dreams when I was much younger: I began walking in slow motion. I was struggling and struggling and using every ounce of effort to move forward, but still I was moving in slow motion.

My problem got so bad that I fell onto the street and I was crawling, just grasping at the ground and trying to pull myself forward. I didn't seem to be getting anywhere. I was making very little progress. I inched my way forward slowly. Meanwhile, Woody and Diane were, of course, getting farther and farther away.

The pedestrian light started blinking: "DON'T WALK, DON'T WALK." Still, I could only crawl. Then the "DON'T WALK" stopped flashing and it came on and stayed there. Cars began honking at me and inching toward me, blaring their horns. There was nothing I could do but just keep trying to crawl, and I started screaming at the cars: "I'm trying! I'm trying!"

I was still just moving in slow motion, with Woody and Diane getting very far away from me, when I woke up from my dream.

Stephen's dream is similar to Jason Weil's dream in that, in spite of struggling, he doesn't catch up with Dream Woody. Woody Allen has been a strong inspiration and model for Stephen in his waking life. But he is a model of someone who excels in communicating attitudes Stephen already holds. That is, Stephen didn't take his outlook on life from Allen. Rather, he used his identification with the artist to expand his own world. Stephen says this dream stimulated him to continue setting new goals for himself, both in terms of artistic efforts and in terms of self-imposed challenges to his developing integrity.

Some might be discouraged by a frustrating dream like Stephen's. But those with high self-esteem can acknowledge a gap between their own achievements and those of others without feeling diminished by that difference. For that reason it is often high self-esteem, I think, that accounts for their ability to identify constructively with a famous or accomplished person.

What happens when a fan does catch up with Dream Woody? Jason Weil was successful in catching up with Woody Allen in the following dream, which he had several years after his first.

———————— LIVING WOODY'S LIFE ————————

I went to see Woody Allen play the clarinet at Michael's Pub. Afterward I followed him home. I managed to sneak up to his penthouse suite without being detected en route.

I knocked on Woody's door. He answered and we made our introductions. He was sad, going through a period of his life where he was fed up with the public. Then, as we continued to talk, Woody got a brain flash: I could become an extension of him! What he meant was that I would be the public Woody. He would continue to write and create as usual. But I would be the Woody who would act in films and deal with the public. It was just what I had always wanted: to be right in the limelight!

We did it. Woody completely faded out of pictures. I began playing at Michael's Pub. It was never clear to me whether people realized that I wasn't really Woody. But it was successful. I made a couple of Woody Allen movies. And we went on like this for slightly over two years—me living the life I'd always wanted to live. And then it happened: suddenly I hated it! I despised it all.

I went to Woody. "I want out," I told him with desperation.

"Now you understand," Woody nodded, and he furrowed his brow before he added: "But it's too late. You have to just keep going."

This dream of personal disillusionment strengthened Jason's empathy with Woody Allen. Jason feels the dream proved to him that Allen's complaints about the burdens of public life are sincere, and that the burdens are all the more overwhelming because they're inescapable.

Stephen Wohl also caught up with Dream Woody. His dream career seems to have progressed in the following dream.

_____ BELONGING TO THE CLUB _____

Woody and Cavett and Steve Martin and I were sitting in a hotel lobby near a revolving door. And as people came through the revolving door we made insulting remarks to them.

The four of us were being loud and obnoxious. So much so that eventually the hotel manager came over and told us that we'd better leave the premises. So, in return, we made insulting remarks to the manager too!

We knew what we were doing was really okay, because there was a comic convention in town and we were all taking part in it! Thus we figured that when the manager read the article in the newspaper about the convention, he'd say to himself: "Oh, why that was Woody Allen and Dick Cavett and Steve Martin and Stephen Wohl! Well, no wonder!"

We did leave the lobby, though, and headed on over to the convention. There was a series of escalators at the convention hall. I started going up one escalator and before long it flattened out until it was just a moving walk like they have in airports.

I looked around me. The people who'd come to the convention were dressed really weird. Many of them were in punk-rock outfits and they had their hair dyed strange colors. Others had on even more obscure outfits. I began to have second thoughts about participating in the convention. I had thought the convention was going to be something really worthwhile. But seeing all of these strangely attired people made me think it was just a publicity stunt. But then I remembered that I, of course, was wearing my ape suit.

I walked into a room where a meeting was in process. It was a planning meeting for the convention. "My God," I thought. "The convention's starting today and they're just now planning it!" I was becoming really upset thinking how poorly organized this affair was.

To top it off, the next thing I knew, someone at the planning meeting whipped out some drugs—Quaaludes, I think. "Shit," I thought. "Now they're all going to get high; they're not taking this seriously."

I was frustrated and upset. I saw this really wonderful thing just start to fall apart. Slowly I started to realize: "This is not going to be how I thought it was."

Stephen, too, was disillusioned by his experiences as a comedian peer of Woody and friends. In a dream, the image

of ascending an escalator often reflects an expansive attitude of high expectations, but Stephen's escalator flattened out as he neared his destination, suggesting that he already suspected things wouldn't be as he had hoped.

Stephen says that the dream was true to life in that he is often angered when other people don't take their work seriously enough. Stephen appreciates the way real-life Woody Allen is meticulous in his attention to details. And he thinks his frustration in the dream would be the way Allen would react to similar events. He is probably right. The serious-mindedness and the aversion to drugs and pop-culture fads sound like Allen, as does Stephen's contradiction: ". . . then I remembered that I, of course, was wearing my ape suit." Allen, too, occasionally undermines his own opportunities to be taken seriously. Once, for instance, he wore sneakers with his tuxedo when he escorted the first lady, Mrs. Ford, to the ballet. Some would consider that stunt to be merely Allen's way of underscoring the fact that he's a professional comedian or an eccentric, or just a publicity gimmick. My own guess is that the sneakers had more to do with two other factors, the first being Allen's desire to deflate the significance of authority figures. Remember distraught Alvy Singer in *Annie Hall* ripping up his driver's license in response to a policeman's demand that he pick it up and give it to him: "I have a terrific problem with authority, you know. I'm—It's not your fault. Don't take it personal." Real-life Allen expressed a similarly rebellious attitude about his school years. "My teachers all loathed me," he told William Zinsser in 1963. "I never did homework—I mean I never *ever* did homework. I'm amazed to this day that they really expected me to go home and work on those sleazy projects that they had outlined. My father and mother were called to school so often that my friends still recognize them on the street."

Second, the sneakers may have come out of Allen's difficulty in resisting the humorous possibilities of the occasion, though with hindsight he might have wished he had curbed his humor, as he has occasionally done in other ways. He no longer perpetuates his image as a comedian by participating in television talk shows, for instance, and engages primarily in serious, philosophical dialogue in interviews with reporters, and of course he has controlled the humor in comedies such as *Annie Hall* and *Manhattan*, in order to increase the dimensions of the characters. Allen's career aspirations involve spending less and less time doing comedy. "Tragedy," he told Natalie Gittelson in a 1979 interview for *The New York Times Magazine*, "is a form to which I would ultimately like to aspire. I tend to prefer it to comedy."

Stephen Wohl's longtime identification with Allen may now be apporaching a destructive edge. Stephen's verbal humor, as seen in the scenario for a possible feature film he is writing, for example, so closely approximates Allen's that it often seems derivative. It remains to be seen whether or not Stephen's work will become limited by that part of his inner world that he shares with Woody Allen.

Woody Allen is renowned among his fellow professionals for his fastidiousness. By the accounts of people who've worked with him, Allen is exacting, demanding, straightforward, controlling, businesslike and always serious. He is particular about all the details of his work, even those of peripheral matters. These qualities come across strongly in this collection of dreams.

•

PATTY JACOBS is a social-work student who has seen Woody Allen twice in real life: once on a street filming *Manhattan* and once at the airport, getting into an old Bentley. Patty, who is an Ingmar Bergman fan, has always liked Allen, but she says he became special to her after she saw *Interiors*. Her dream is from October 10, 1980.

FASTIDIOUS WOODY

I was typing Woody's newest script for him while he sat right at my side. We were in a dark, modern office—his office. We got along famously. But Woody had definite ideas about spacing. He wanted a quality product and he was going to make sure that was what he got. So he just sat there next to me, holding his finger to his cheek, tilting his head to the side, and checking my spacing.

Patty is confident that her dream portrays real-life Allen accurately: that he knows what he wants in his work and is very serious about it, but that he can also be patient and friendly with people who work for him. Unlike some of Allen's real-life coworkers who occasionally find his perfectionism to be a pain in the neck, Patty enjoyed the close attention of Dream Woody. She woke up from the dream excited and happy because of the new connection she felt with the artist.

In showing Dream Woody's extreme concern with her spacing—i.e., with the aesthetic appearance of her work—Patty's dream also indirectly reflects real-life Allen's attention to visual images. The visual gags and other images in his films are memorable. Take, for example, Miles Monroe in *Sleeper*, wearing his inflatable flying outfit and soaring through the air with the force and grace of a balloon in Macy's Thanksgiving Day parade or his schizoid robot's uniform; or Gene Wilder in *Everything You Always Wanted to Know About Sex* (*But Were Afraid to Ask)* as the dejected Dr. Ross who, having lost his true love, a sheep, is seen in a skid row, slouched against the curb, red-faced, drinking from a bottle of Woolite; or Sidney Finklestein's furry Hostility, unleashed and rampaging through the woods in *Stardust Memories*. And consider the visual splendor of Allen's *Manhattan, Interiors* and *A Midsummer Night's Sex Comedy* and the extraordinary visual creations in *Zelig,* all with Gordon Willis's photography.

•

TED LASSER is a twenty-one-year-old theatrical booking agent who grew up in Bayside. Woody Allen appeals to Ted "because of his standards as a writer and a producer—because he does what he really wants to do." Ted is shy: "I like to keep myself secret.... Woody and I are on the same wavelength. There'd be an equal understanding between us if we ever spoke." Ted has never dreamed about other celebrities, but his dream about Woody occurred five times in 1978 and 1979.

WHY A DUCK?

I was working as a waiter in the back section of a nice restaurant when who should come strolling in but Woody Allen and two beautiful, snobbish, smoking models. The models were thin, with high cheekbones and dark hair like lovely French models. Now, I took my work seriously: I was a professional waiter, and as stiff as one could be. So I didn't even let on that I recognized Woody Allen. I seated the three of them against a wall, and as I did so I overheard Woody boasting to the models about what a good place this was. I recommended the roast lamb, the duck and the breaded chicken breasts and then I took their orders. "This is a good place," Woody reassured the two women again, and then when he must have thought I was out of earshot, I heard him say: "That fellow must have been a train conductor somewhere."

Five minutes later, I was back at their table, bringing a big tray with a giant knife and fork. Woody looked aghast, but the models remained indifferent. "This place has a big reputation," Woody said.

Then I came back out, leading a lamb on a leash, and I tied it to their table. "That's the first time I've seen a live birth-control device!'' Woody quipped. But I remained professional. I was just doing my job.

I returned then with a live duck and a live chicken and placed them, squawking, on plates in front of the models. Woody was embarrassed, to say the least. "Is there anything more I can get you?'' I asked.

"I think these are a tad undercooked,'' Woody said.

That enraged me! And I replied in a very haughty way: "Well, I'm very, very sorry! I can just take them back to where they came from, if that's how you feel about it!''

"Just give me the billl,'' Woody said.

"That's why I gave you the duck,'' I said angrily.

He was angry, too. "I've had enough,'' he said. He collected his models and started away from the table.

I was dumbfounded. I'd really put myself out for them. "Where's my tip?'' I yelled after them.

Woody turned right around and looked back at me. He pointed a finger for emphasis as he spoke. "If you want to find a good tip, find a good rabbi,'' he said.

Ted says that in his waking life he is an overproducer: he tries too hard. "I always fear I'm not doing enough," he says. Each time Ted has this dream, in which he clearly outdoes himself, he is reminded of his problem. Ted doesn't completely understand what he's overcompensating for but feels he gets closer to that insight each time he has this dream. The extent of his "overproducing" is emphasized for him in the dream by the fact that his efforts were overkill even to a diligent worker like Woody Allen.

But Ted's dream also reveals an aggressively competitive interest in Allen. Part of the reason Ted doesn't acknowledge recognizing Woody in the restaurant may be that Ted's a serious, professional waiter, but an even greater motivating factor seems to be his desire to diminish the significance of Allen's fame. Ted's serving of live entrées and his other shocking behavior as a waiter seem aimed at embarrassing Dream Woody in front of his guests, whom Dream Woody is eager to please. Dream Woody handles the indignities imposed upon him much as real-life Allen does: by using humor to express his anger. Dream Woody even saves his best quip for his exiting line: "If you want to find a good tip, find a good rabbi."

•

JED STEIN is a retail salesperson, a writer and a native New Yorker. He and Woody Allen share many interests, including Russian literature, humor and playing the clarinet. Allen is the only celebrity Jed has dreamed about who isn't a political activist. Jed's other celebrity dream objects include Joan Baez, Julian Bond and George McGovern. His one Woody dream is from January 31, 1979.

_____ **WHAT'S MY LINE?** _____

My woman friend and I were in the studio audience of the TV show "What's My Line?" Woody Allen was the guest host that night. I was impressed with Woody. He was charming and witty, although his humor might be said to be obscure. A panelist sitting next to Arlene Francis addressed a question to Woody: "Are you happy?"

"To find out, I'll need a philanderist!" Woody quipped.

"Oh? And what is a philanderist?" the panelist said, chuckling afterward.

"A European theologian!" was Woody's quick comeback. Woody was one great host! He was straight-faced and composed through the whole show. I couldn't stop admiring how smooth, how competent he was.

Jed says that his dream reflects his waking-life opinion that Woody Allen is an especially literate and commanding artist. As in Ted Lasser's dream, the Woody of Jed's dream also manages to interject some striking, if obscure, one-liners.

Woody in Jed's dream seems to be evading the topic of romance. When he first says he needs a philanderist to find out if he's happy, Dream Woody seems to be saying he needs an expert on romance. But when a panelist tries to pursue the issue, Dream Woody cleverly gives the word a new slant and avoids further probing of the topic. This is consistent with real-life Allen, who shuns discussing his personal life and particularly his love life in interviews. He generally accomplishes this by a careful selection of whom he grants interviews to, but he is also skilled at terminating topics he doesn't want to discuss (obviously, a vital skill for anyone in the public eye). In his 1974 interview with Leonard Probst at the New School, for instance, Allen called on a dignified-looking, fiftyish woman with a pleasant smile who rose from her seat in the audience and said with total seriousness: "Mr. Allen, could you tell us what kind of sexual perversions you have?" The question did not receive an answer.

•

DOUG WATSON is a New York taxi driver who has struggled to give up a life of crime and who now aspires to be a filmmaker. Doug, who used to be a heavy drinker, has led a traumatic life. "I grew up in a few jail cells. I'm used to jail. Jail don't bother me, but it's a horrible place to be. It's a hellhole, let's put it that way." He used to be a drug dealer, making as much as five thousand dollars a day. During that period of his life he was recruited to be a professional killer. He turned down the offer to be a hit man and eventually quit dealing drugs and took a legitimate job.

Doug sees Woody Allen as someone who's been "a comedian and a nut" but who always really wanted to be serious. Doug says that he, too, has always been able to make people laugh, but that now he also wants to be serious. Doug had the following dream on his third night in jail on a trumped-up assault charge.

─────────── WOODY OR THE BABY ───────────

Woody Allen and I were looking over a set of New York on the water. We were considering the set for a movie that we were making together. But while we were looking it over, we started arguing.

I was trying to produce a soul group. But Woody didn't want the soul group in our movie. And so we were arguing and arguing about it. He knew what he wanted and what he didn't want. I remember Woody's face: it was very, very serious.

I was really upset. He was determined not to have the group. And so at some point I just turned away from him.

When I turned away from Woody, I saw a baby running down the hallway. He was too young to be able to walk, but from nowhere he was running at me. And he leaped from the floor to my neck and started ripping at my head.

The baby was trying to kill me. I was screaming and desperately trying to pull it from my neck.

Finally I ripped the thing off my neck and I killed it. And then I woke up from my dream, screaming.

The inmates were all calling me names. But all I said to them was: "I just had a dream about some soul singers."

Doug has heard the myth that when you die in a dream, you die in real life. So he experienced his dream as literally a life-and-death battle. "This baby was trying to rip my neck right out of my socket, you understand. I was fighting for my life in my dream." His dream does seem, symbolically, to represent a fight for his life. Doug has an enormous amount of undirected mental energy. In his dream, he tried, as he is trying in his waking life, to focus that energy on filmmaking. He was trying to be serious and directed like Dream Woody. But when he turned away and lost that focus just for a second, he found himself about to be destroyed. Doug is creative and energetic, but, as he says, "The hell's demon's in my system."

In contrast to the self-control and direction symbolized by Dream Woody, the baby in Doug's dream can be seen as representing the demon in his system: his earlier, more primal and destructive origins. The demon went straight for Doug's head, signifying that Doug's demise would come from a loss of his rational control. On the surface, Doug's dream seems to contrast with other dreams in which Woody Allen is seen as a guide to the unconscious, rather than to greater rational control. But that could be the basis for Doug's unconscious choice of Allen in his dream; that is, Doug experiences Allen as someone who reaches into his unconscious without sacrificing rational control. Regardless, Doug's conquering the demon in his system will be dependent on his keeping his focus on being serious, respecting himself, and persevering, even when there's conflict, as there was in his dream between himself and Dream Woody.

Persevering is an important part of Allen's commitment to his art. Woody Allen has been working diligently at his creations, with no apparent time out, since he was a teenager. The enormous growth of his craft over the years reflects his unrelenting effort, as well as his particular attention to detail. In describing Allen's influence on their careers, the men and women interviewed for this book repeatedly referred to "sticking to it," "not letting others influence you" and "taking yourself seriously." Allen's colleague and friend Marshall Brickman also credits Allen with encouraging him to take himself seriously as an artist. Allen once told Brickman that if you present yourself as an artist, other people will treat you like one. He gives similar advice in the following dreams.

•

LOU FINKLESTEIN is a psychotherapist who thinks of Woody Allen as a personal guru that he's never met. Lou appreciates Allen's phenomenological world view, and his only criticism of him is that he is a classicist. "Why, for instance," Lou asks, "couldn't Tracy, at the end of *Manhattan*, have been getting a taxi instead of a limo?" The following is one of at least three dreams Lou has had about Allen.

DEAR WOODY

I was at that stage of my doctoral dissertation where I was blocked, and I was considering giving up on it. I went to discuss the matter with my graduate adviser, Woody Allen.

I went to Allen's apartment for the meeting. He was wearing tan fatigues and a corduroy shirt with a sweater over it. I noticed that he also had on Adidas sneakers and white socks.

I had expected him to have psychoanalytic journals in his apartment. Instead he had a lot of magazines and stacks of *The New York Review of Books*. He served me health foods as we talked.

Woody began by urging me to persevere with my dissertation. He then stressed that I should also stick with my "existential, phenomenological view of life." Woody told me that there really is something to live for and that I should look to my future with hope. "Your work is important," he said to me.

Woody was very much into the issue of personal liberties. Consequently, we spent a great deal of time discussing Thomas Szasz and mental illness.

As we talked, I could feel Woody's sensitivity and tenderness toward other people. I could sense his concern for social problems. And Woody, in turn, was able to feel my concern for the problems of all humanity.

I later went for a second appointment with Woody. He was dressed the same this time, except that he now was wearing dark sweat socks. Once more, Woody encouraged me to persevere and to keep my phenomenological outlook. Woody empathized with me completely, even with my problem in meeting women.

The details in Lou's dream capture the spirit, if not the facts, of real-life Allen. I don't know of any accounts of Allen's being into health foods per se, but the health foods in Lou's dream do reflect Allen's stoicism. (Dream Woody feeding Lou health foods also supports his role as nurturer in the dream.) The fact that Dream Woody only changed socks is consistent with the public image of Allen always wearing the same kind of clothes: casual and baggy with sneakers. Dream Woody's concern with personal liberties is also true of the filmmaker. Dream Woody apparently had a special concern for the personal liberties of mental-health patients: Thomas Szasz is the psychiatrist who put forth the thesis that mental illness is a myth (*The Myth of Mental Illness*, 1961, and *The Manufacture of Madness*, 1970). Real-life Allen is particularly involved with trying to prevent censorship in the arts.

Lou's straightforward dream inspired him to complete his doctoral dissertation and to continue expanding his world view. It also helped him to feel more accepting about the difficulty he has finding a good relationship with a woman. He thinks the Woody Allen of his dream is no different from real-life Woody and that in fact Allen would make an excellent college professor and graduate school adviser.

•

JET CLAREY is a cartoon artist who owns an original Woody Allen doodling. Jet saw Allen speak as a member of a panel at a counterjournalism convention in 1974. Jet arrived in the convention auditorium early and left a note on the podium for Allen, requesting an autograph and a chance to talk with him after the panel. Jet didn't get to speak to Allen. When he went back to the podium to retrieve his note after everyone had left he discovered no autograph from Allen, but a page covered with doodlings, including three apparent self-portraits and the slogan "existential death." Jet sees Allen as one of the most important filmmakers alive, whose work has "progressed and matured till it is now beyond satire." The dream below is from the night of the convention in 1974.

─────────────── **COMIC INSIGHT** ───────────────

I was walking through a big field like the ones where rock concerts are usually held. There were a lot of people and we were all walking along in the same direction. Bob Hope, Groucho Marx and Woody Allen were near me. Ahead of us were the rolling hills.

We came to a small self-contained room, and Hope, Marx and Allen ushered me in. "We've brought you here with us in order to advise you," Woody gently told me.

Jet says this is one of the few dreams he's given much thought to. It made him feel optimistic about his future. People often find confirmation of what they want to do by receiving advice or reassurance in a dream from someone they respect. And the tone of Jet's dream suggests even more than advice: it seems that Jet is being initiated into this small group of people whom he admires. Jet thinks of the dream as a premonition of his move, shortly thereafter, from his Irish Catholic home in Boston to Hollywood to begin his career.

•

BLUE WARREN is a graphic artist who grew up in the San Fernando Valley. He records his dreams almost every day as a form of self-discovery, and he had a dream about Woody Allen just three days before hearing about this study. Blue appreciates Allen's aloneness in the city and respects him for being "completely honest—to a masochistic degree." His dream is from March 19, 1980.

WOODY'S SECRET

Woody Allen found me a New York bungalow apartment for $210 to $250 a month. What a deal! It even had a view of the suburbs. An overweight, Jewish, motherly friend of Woody's took care of the arrangements. "This is all yours; do you like it?" she asked me as I walked around my new place.

"Like it— are you kidding? This is so great I can't believe it!" I replied. Then I quickly composed myself, thinking that the real estate guy might up the price if he heard from her how much I liked the place.

As good as this was, though, the great thing was I was going to meet Woody Allen! *He* contacted *me*: I kept saying it over and over to make myself believe it. I could still hear his words from that telephone call. "I've got a big plan, but I don't want to tell you yet," Woody said.

Woody suggested that he, Marshall Brickman and I meet together in San Francisco at a gay club, where Woody was going to give a talk.

"Sure," I said. "I'm not gay, but I don't mind going there."

I've been a holdout most of my life. I could have done more comedy, but I wanted to protect my integrity. And now, even with my minimal exposure, Woody and Marshall Brickman had heard about me. "They want me!" I kept thinking. "I'm funny and they know it."

On our way to the meeting in San Francisco, we stopped at a place where I wouldn't really have minded working, even though it was a dungeon. It was a pure white dungeon with no plants and it was at the bottom of a gully. But the sun went all the way down into the gully. My only concern was that during rainy times it might get flooded.

But Woody nixed my working there. "No, you'd get depressed here," he told me. I followed his intuition. I felt just great because Woody was giving me the things that I've never been able to give myself: organizational ability, for example.

"We'll help each other," Woody said, as though reading my thoughts.

It was all such a wonderful experience. Still, at the end of this very busy day, one thought returned to haunt me: "Woody Allen gay? Of course, it all makes sense now. This must be one of Hollywood's best kept secrets."

In his dream, Blue, too, is being initiated into an exclusive group of individuals he admires. Blue felt "more empathy with Allen as a creative person" after this dream. And he felt encouraged as a result of Dream Woody nurturing him. The dream, Blue says, meant that he was being rewarded for not selling out. "Allen hasn't gone against his own conscience and he saw that I hadn't, either."

What about Woody's secret? According to Blue, this symbolized his fear that Woody Allen's motives are not as noble as he believes them to be—that Allen is perhaps, sometimes hypocritical. Blue still believes Allen is honest, but he's watching the artist more closely now—in case his dream was onto something.

It may be that Blue has projected onto Dream Woody concerns about himself, whether about homosexuality or something symbolized by homosexuality. The dungeon at the bottom of the gully might have provided Blue with an opportunity to be alone and confront himself directly. There were no distractions there—not even plants, and the life-giving sun reached all the way into the dungeon. Thus, Blue's concern about being flooded represents his fear of too much contact with his unconscious. He was still willing to give the dungeon a try but Dream Woody discouraged him. Unlike Woody's role in other dreams, in which he serves as a guide to the unconscious, in this dream Woody seems to be protecting Blue from his unconscious instead of pushing him to probe further. The dream could be interpreted as meaning that Dream Woody recognized what Blue didn't: that Blue was not ready for the dungeon. Or perhaps Blue's dream reflects his desire to avoid confronting: his search for a rationalization, which is provided by Dream Woody. "Even Woody Allen"—whom Blue has described as being "completely honest—to a masochistic degree"—"has secrets," seems to be the dream's theme.

Collaboration with Woody on an artistic project and sharing professional experiences appeared as a theme in several dreams.

•

ANN WEIDE is a title searcher in downtown New York. Ann loves comedy and uses it as her defense mechanism. "I relate to Woody's comic way of relating to serious things in life; it's very Jewish." Ann respects Allen for his integrity, his commitment to privacy, and because "he doesn't downgrade anybody but himself." The dream below is from 1974.

———————— MUTUAL INTERESTS ————————

I wrote a novel which Woody was interested in. He therefore arranged to come to my apartment to discuss it with me.

When Woody arrived at my apartment, another friend of mine, a man, was present. The friend let Woody in because I was in the other room practicing my clarinet. So the first thing Woody learned when he arrived was that I can play the clarinet, too.

I was very nervous. It was Sunday and I had made brunch. I had lox and bagels. I was especially nervous because I know how shy Woody is, and I wanted badly to respect that. I kept saying things to him like: "Eat something? Would you like some lox and bagels? I'll make you an egg cream!"

Woody was nice—shy but articulate. It was a very business-like get-together: we were just collaborating as two writers do. Nothing else.

The novel I had written involved Siamese twins, and in the movie version that Woody and I created, he and I played the Siamese twins. The movie focuses on how being a Siamese twin can affect one's sexual roles. Since Woody and I both play the clarinet, we made the twins musicians.

We wrote the film and then we shot it. I could visualize it clearly in my dream: the two of us, as Siamese twins, playing our clarinets. I woke up feeling inspired to work on my creative side.

Ann's dream embodies her wish to be close to Woody Allen: as Dream Woody's Siamese twin, she is as close to him as anyone could be. Her unconscious pun ("I woke up feeling inspired to work on my creative side") reveals the aspect of her personality Woody represents. Ann hadn't been working on her "creative side" before this dream. But the fact that, in her dream, somebody she really respects accepted her potential encouraged her to do the same. Ann had always longed to be a filmmaker, and she began her first course in film shortly after this dream.

•

MERLE GLAUBMAN is a film teacher whose favorite film-maker is Godard. In her waking life, Merle has seen Woody Allen three times: twice at John's Pizzeria on Bleecker Street and once on Thompson Street, also in Greenwich Village. Merle sees Allen as a contradiction: "a human, accessible professional," but also "an inaccessible, media-hype director." Her dream is from spring 1977.

_____ CINEMA (CHUCKLE) STUDIES _____

I looked out the window of my Soho apartment into the courtyard below, my courtyard. There was a group of people investigating the space. One of the people was Woody Allen.

I knew what this was all about. They were a group of investors hoping to buy out the space to build a small cabaret.

I opened the window, walked out onto my fire escape and yelled angrily: "You're not going to put a restaurant back here! Don't you see how it would affect the people living in this building?

"I don't care who you are," I added angrily. "You're not going to put a restaurant here!"

Everyone in the group looked concerned. One of the investors spoke up: "We'll come up and talk to you about it."

The man who had spoken and Woody Allen came up to my apartment.

"Can we come in?" Woody asked as I opened the door.

I think he disliked me because of my anger.

I motioned for them both to sit down in my kitchen. I sat down, too. They spoke almost in unison: "Let's be a little bit more reasonable. What are your feelings about a restaurant in the back?"

I explained my complaint to them. "Look," I said. "This is my kitchen. I work in my kitchen. This is where my best light is."

Then Woody inquired: "Well, what do you do?"

"I teach film at the university," I told him.

"Ooh, you do!" Woody said, appearing quite interested now.

"In the Department of Cinema Studies," I added.

"What do you *do* in Cinema Studies?" Woody asked with an emphasis that suggested that it was a mystery he had been pondering at length.

"If you're interested in knowing, you can come to one of my classes," I replied. I was cavalier because I was on my own turf.

I went on. "You'd probably be interested in the way in which film students and untrained viewers learn film. I could tell you some interesting stories.''

"Yeah, like what?" Woody said, with just a trace of antagonism.

"For instance," I said. "I'm grading midterms now. And some of my students have funny misassumptions about spelling. One student, for example, was writing an answer to an essay question about high-angle shots. Only she misspelled 'angle': she spelled it 'angel.' And eventually her wires became crossed from this misspelling, so that she began to conceive of the term as though it were 'high-angel.' On her essay she wrote that it was 'as though from the point of view of God.'

"Then what is a low-angel shot?" I wrote back on her midterm.

I decided to share another funny story with Woody. My anger had dissipated as soon as I saw that he was interested in my work.

"Another student of mine," I told Woody, "was writing about the debate of Soviet filmmakers on editing theory. One Soviet filmmaker says that putting together a film is like putting together links in a chain. Another filmmaker says the relationship of shot to shot is like two pieces that collide. Thus the debate is between linkage and collision."

Woody looked intent on what I was saying.

"So one of my students," I continued, "was writing about Pudovkin. And he wrote: 'Pudovkin was into linkage.' ''

"Okay," Woody said. "I'll come to your film class."

Then, after thinking a moment, he rephrased his earlier question: "But how do you teach movies?"

"You can come to my class," was my only reply.

"I don't want anybody to recognize me," Woody said with a sudden look of concern. "I don't want to make a big deal about this!"

My classroom is at the end of a long corridor. Along both sides of the corridor are the offices of all the film teachers and other workers.

Woody came with me to the class. He walked along behind me as we walked down the long corridor to my room. Woody had the collar of his green fatigue coat turned up and he had his hands in his pockets and he was trying hard to be as unobtrusive as possible.

As we walked along the corridor we could hear the whispers of people in the offices:

"Do you see who that is with Merle?"

"Isn't that Woody Allen?"

"Look—look who's out there!"

"My God, that's Woody Allen, isn't it?"

And finally, a conclusive:

"No! That isn't Woody Allen. It just looks like him."

"Aah."

Merle bridged somewhat the gap between the inaccessible and the accessible Woody Allen in her dream. By being self-confident in her own professionalism, Merle led Dream Woody to become interested in her work, even to the extent of wanting to learn from her. Dream Woody's initial antagonism toward film studies reflects a sentiment often heard from Allen. In his story "The Lunatic's Tale," for example, he praises a woman for having "the appropriate hostility toward all deserving targets: politicians, television, facelifts, the architecture of housing projects, men in leisure suits, film courses, and people who begin sentences with 'basically.' "

As Alvy in *Annie Hall*, Allen says: "You know, you know how you're always tryin' t' get things to come out perfect in art because, uh, it's real difficult in life." In his work, Allen creates from his inner world, takes risks, regards himself seriously, perseveres and attends to detail. It's easy to understand why fans who take their own work seriously have chosen Woody Allen as a model for artistic integrity. The next dream shows what happens when a fan is fickle about her professional commitments.

•

NINA JAFFIN is an art therapist: she helps patients get in touch with, express and clarify their feelings by expressing them through art. Nina expresses ambivalence about a number of things in her life, including New York and Woody Allen movies. She had the following dream early in the fall of 1979.

_____ **FROM STAR TO SHRINK** _____

I was in Philadelphia, where I was starring in a Woody Allen film. I had just left rehearsal. I was feeling good. The shooting had gone well, and I had enjoyed every moment of it. It was an up day all around.

I walked along the street away from the studio. The studio was in a business area and there were quite a few people on the streets, although the streets were not as crowded as they would be in a similar area of New York.

I came to a red-brick store-restaurant complex and I approached a revolving door. As I was headed toward the revolving door, a doctor I knew was headed out that door.

I waited a moment just to say hello to him even though he is, in fact, someone I do not like. The doctor gave me a broad smile and a big hello, both of which were very unusual. Ordinarily, he doesn't acknowledge me at all. I noted that he was with a strikingly attractive woman.

Much to my surprise, the doctor immediately offered me a truly great job in art therapy. With no hesitation, I said: "Great, fine. I'll take it. Wonderful! I'll quit the Woody Allen film at once, because this—art therapy—is what I really want to do with my life."

I said good-bye to the doctor and then headed in through the revolving door. I was on my way to an analysis session, and I turned my attention now to looking for the office of my new analyst, Dick Cavett.

Had the dream continued, Nina's new analyst might have taken a dim view of her impulsive dumping of her starring role in Woody Allen's film, since, in real life, Cavett and Allen are close friends. The fact that Nina is going to see another "Woody representative" for guidance suggests she doesn't trust her decision. After all, her outstanding job offer came from a doctor who usually doesn't even speak to her. Nina's revolving-door dream suggested to her that she needs to give more thought to what she really wants in life.

Man to Man

Almost all of the dreamers want to be friends with Dream Woody. The desire to get to know him better, to be closer and to share with him, is an important theme in most of the dreams. But some of the dreamers feel that before they can be close to Allen they need to do something to impress him.

The desire to impress Woody Allen is seen in both the men's and the women's dreams. However, men's dreams often reveal a competitive edge to the desire to impress.

•

LEE SCHULTZ is a thirty-two-year-old shiatsu masseur with a strong interest in baking and cooking nutritious food. He thinks that he and Woody Allen were connected in a previous life—that they may have been brothers. Lee respects Allen's work but hopes the filmmaker will "go more toward happy, optimistic pictures." Lee has great trust in his intuition and relies on it to direct his life. His intuition tells him that he will one day meet Woody Allen.

TIME OUT

I was playing basketball in a park in Manhattan. Woody was nearby dribbling a ball. Suddenly he dribbled over to me. "Want to play one on one with me?" he asked.

I was so surprised that I started to laugh. "You mean you're not busy now?" I said.

We played together for about fifteen minutes. I was really hot! I was way ahead of Woody: he hadn't scored a basket yet. He was tired and red in the face. He got the ball again, and then he called time out. Then, straight-faced, he added: "I'm calling time out till Tuesday."

"Let's go get something to eat," Woody said.

At my urging we went to a macrobiotic restaurant. Woody was apprehensive. "I don't want to take my shoes off," he told me.

"Don't worry," I said.

The waitress brought us tempura and tofu and miso and sake. Woody found all of these to be quite unusual.

I thought Woody needed a little more nutritionwise, and so I asked him: "Why don't you try and change your eating habits just a little bit?"

"Why? What's it done for you?" Woody retorted.

That was a good question. I had to stop and think about it for a while.

After some thought, I explained to Woody that since changing my eating habits, I felt more peaceful and less anxious, less frustrated.

"Sure," Woody said. "But you haven't had a job in four years."

"That's true, but I still feel better," I insisted.

Next, Woody and I were in a hotel room in the middle of a self-development class. I had managed to talk Woody into going there even though he kept making jokes about it. "After all, I've been in therapy twenty-three years," he kept telling me.

Then something surprising occurred. It was Woody's turn to talk in the group and something came over him! He began releasing all of these deep, deep feelings that he'd had for a very long time: feelings so deep that he couldn't express them to his private therapist. As all of these feelings came to the surface Woody felt vulnerable, but still he continued—with the support of the group.

Finally, Woody ended up with an entirely different perspective on himself. He looked as though he had lost about one hundred pounds of energy in his head area. He smiled more. And I, of course, smiled too, because I was so happy at Woody's growth.

Woody put his arm around me, and he didn't really say anything, but I understood his unspoken word. As this scene drew to a close, Woody began to explain to me how much more positive he felt about everything, and especially about his relationships with women.

Lee experienced his dream as being about "mutual love." He and Dream Woody became close friends, and Lee was able to nurture him the way he says he would like to nurture real-life Allen (and the way, perhaps, he would like to nurture aspects of his own personality). Were the dream to continue, it seems likely that Dream Woody would be well on his way to making the "happy, optimistic pictures" that Lee wants to see, movies like Allen's *A Midsummer Night's Sex Comedy,* which came after Lee's dream.

Lee's dream captures the confrontational style—more or less a friendly anatgonism—seen between the characters Allen portrays in his pictures and their respective friends. Dream Woody doesn't let Lee off the hook easily. In defense of his eating habits, Lee explained to Dream Woody that he felt "more peaceful and less anxious, less frustrated." "Sure," Dream Woody said. "But you haven't had a job in four years."

Several of these dreams show Woody Allen's desire for privacy, and Dream Woody's reluctance in Lee's dream to remove his shoes can also be seen as his resistance to revealing his personal life—before the group experience in which he released all his pent-up feelings.

•

MICHAEL KLAPMAN is a thirty-nine-year-old psychologist turned video-game inventor. Michael is a competitive man who first became active in sports in his early thirties and now takes great pride in his athletic achievements. He says he greatly admires Woody Allen's work but has no interest in the artist's personality or personal life.

_____ QUALITY BALLS _____

I was in a paddle-ball court waiting to play. It was a brand-new hall and a brand-new court. As I waited for my turn to play, I thought about the little black balls that people play paddle ball with. There's a shortage of these little black balls now and everyone is speculating why. I was trying to figure out my own theory.

As I waited, another player approached me and explained to me that now there were four kinds of balls! The kind of ball you used was based on how well you played. He explained that the number on the can that the balls come in gives the quality of the ball and furthermore that only players at a corresponding level of quality in their game can use those balls.

I contemplated this new information as I continued to wait my turn to play. Then I glanced over at a court two courts down from me and noticed that Woody Allen was playing there. I idly looked at him, noticing that he was somewhat taller and more muscular than I had imagined. I was extremely curious about his athletic ability.

As it turned out, it was clear that Woody was quite athletic. He was very good, and it was pleasurable to watch him play.

I liked the way Woody played so much that I left my court to go see if I could play with him! By this time, however, it was getting dark, and when I arrived at his court it was apparent that it was too dark to play.

I was disappointed that I didn't get to play with Woody. And I also never found out whether I _could_ have played with him, because I didn't get to see what level his balls were.

Michael says that this dream has to do with his dormant awareness of Allen's athletic competency. He was reminded by the dream that, contrary to the early Woody schlep persona, real-life Allen is actually quite athletic. Beyond Michael's interpretation, the dream seems to be a rather transparent comparison of his manhood with that of Dream Woody.

Why Woody Allen? Perhaps because Allen has broken the stereotype of masculinity. He originally became known as a wise, sensitive, comic but nonmacho genius. And he thereby gave men who were not macho in the traditional sense someone to identify with. In later movies (*Annie Hall, Manhattan, Stardust Memories* and *A Midsummer Night's Sex Comedy*), however, Allen presented himself as being athletic, sexually self-confident and popular with women as well. So, for competitive men, Woody Allen has become a rival as well as someone to identify with.

•

DUKE SMITH is a clerk-typist who would like to write, direct and act in films, and to be a stand-up comic. He has met Woody Allen twice: both times at Michael's Pub on East Fifty-fifth Street. Duke had the following dream in the late spring of 1979.

_____ **YOU HAD TO HAVE BEEN THERE** _____

I was in Michael's Pub, behind the rope at the bar. I leaned on the bar and looked into the main dining room. I saw Woody Allen sitting alone on the bandstand. The band was on a break.

A moment later Marshall Brickman came onto the bandstand. He carried a bag of thin pretzels. The two of them sat there munching pretzels and chatting.

Next, I was in Woody's apartment. His apartment, conveniently, was above Michael's Pub. Woody was sitting in a big white fluffy chair: the chair was plush like velour. And I was sitting on the floor at Woody's feet.

A guy walked through Woody's apartment—no one I recognized. Neither of us paid any attention to him. Then the phone rang.

I answered the phone and took a message for Woody. I hung up and handed him the written message.

Then I quipped to Woody: "Him I don't know! Lou Costello, nineteen forty-three."

Woody laughed hysterically at my remark. I had never, but never, seen him laugh that much.

To judge by the way it appears in several of the men's dreams, the ability to make Dream Woody laugh represents the capacity to be taken seriously by him. This stands to reason: the one thing everyone knows about Woody Allen is that he is one of the funniest people alive. And so making *him* laugh seems like a reasonable way to demonstrate affection, as well as to show that the dreamer is a peer of Woody's—that he can do what Woody does.

Duke's dream illustrates a transition from being a fan to being a peer that is common in this collection of dreams. Duke begins his dream behind the rope at the bar at Michael's Pub—in the small area in which, in real life, fans crowd to catch a glimpse of Woody Allen. He then progresses to Dream Woody's apartment, where he first sits on the floor at the filmmaker's feet and then waits on him. Finally, he dares to address Dream Woody as a peer and successfully bowls him over with his wit.

•

PALMER DALTON is an L.A.-based film production assistant who wishes Woody Allen would start a film community as Lucas and Coppola have. Although Palmer rarely remembers dreams, he recalls two about Woody Allen. The following, from 1975, is his first.

FLEXIBLE WOODY

It was another rainy day on campus, and as I walked by the grand-stands I could see a lone figure sitting there in the rain. As I got closer, I could see it was—or looked like—Woody Allen.

"Aren't you Woody Allen?" I asked.

"Yes," he replied. That was all.

I suggested that he come inside. Now I don't mean to imply that Woody Allen didn't know enough to come in out of the rain; it wasn't that way at all: it was just that he was flexible.

I took Woody in, and we sat down and talked while he dried off. No one paid any attention to him sitting there. We talked a long time, and I made Woody laugh a lot.

Palmer, like Duke, "woke up feeling wonderful about making Woody Allen laugh." Bringing Dream Woody in out of the rain also suggests protecting him from his self, literally and symbolically. In dreams rain often symbolizes renewal by increased contact with the unconscious. But Palmer brought Dream Woody back into the mundane world of consciousness, in which he was apparently equally content. This dream suggests a theme that appears often in this collection: that Woody is both a man of the world and a man of the spirit and that he serves as a link between the two.

•

TOM FRAMINGHAM is a twenty-one-year-old visual-arts student who is also developing a career as a pop and blues singer. Tom loves all of Allen's work, including *Stardust Memories,* and identifies with his views on drugs. (Allen said in a 1979 interview with Frank Rich for *Time:* "I've always had a strong feeling about drugs. I don't think it's right to try to buy your way out of life's painful side by using drugs." And in a 1979 interview with Natalie Gittelson for *The New York*

Times Magazine, he criticized show-business people for their use of drugs: "They're a lot of worldly, sophisticated, talented people who seem to be conducting their lives reasonably well—except that they buy out the really tough choices by doping themselves up." Allen's antidrug stance is seen often in his films: in *Annie Hall,* for instance, Alvy reproaches Annie for needing to smoke marijuana to relax for lovemaking; in *Manhattan* Ike argues with a television show's director and producer about whether an episode Ike has written is funny. "There's not a legitimate laugh in that," Ike argues. "All you guys do is-is, uh, drop ludes and then-then take Percodans and angel dust. Naturally, it seems funny." "Relax," the director tells him. But Ike goes on: "Anything would if you're—if you're . . . You know, we, y-y-you should abandon the show and open a pharmaceutical house."

Tom's dream is from November 1980.

THE LADY AND THE VAGRANT

I was walking in a sunny, vivid green park: the park from *Go Ask Alice.* Ahead of me was a picnic table with three individuals. As I got closer to the table I realized that Woody Allen was one of the three! The other two individuals were a middle-aged lady—the type whose children have left home and who is just out taking a walk to kill time—and a vagrant. The lady and the vagrant were drinking and eating.

It was obvious that Woody Allen had supplied the food and the wine. He was trying out new comic material on the lady and the vagrant and on anybody who walked by. But the man and woman were not paying any attention to him. Woody was sitting there, doing his routines, and it was as though he'd been talking their heads off. But the lady and the vagrant were more interested in the food.

As I approached, Woody flagged me in. He raised a glass to

me. "Here, try this—really good wine," he said. "Taylor California rosé!" It was a deep red rosé.

I took a sip and found the wine delicious, which I showed Woody by my expression.

"Sit down; have some cream cheese and bagels," he said. So, I drank and ate, and Woody Allen began to tell me a joke, while the lady and the vagrant still paid no attention.

Woody's joke was about a boy and a girl and the girl's girl-friend. The boy and girl were going to set the friend up on a blind date. The boy said to the girl: "If you feel nervous, just give me this clue." Then Woody gave me the clue—and the clue was the punch line of his joke—but it went right over my head.

What could I do? I couldn't ask him to repeat it! I couldn't say: "I don't get it, Woody!" Woody looked at me expectantly, and my enormous anxiety ended my dream.

I woke up feeling badly that I'd let Woody Allen down, just because of my embarrassment. I got up, went out and bought some Taylor rosé.

It's fitting that this dream is set in the park from *Go Ask Alice*, an antidrug film, since Tom sees eye to eye with Woody Allen on the subject of drugs. Surprisingly, neither Tom nor Dream Woody seems to worry about wine as a drug. (Real-life Allen is not a big drinker. Only in recent years has he developed a taste for wine. In one of his stand-up routines from the sixties Allen explained: "I'm not a drinker, really. My body will not tolerate spirits. I had two martinis New Year's Eve and I tried to hijack an elevator and fly it to Cuba.") Dream Woody's referring to the wine as "Taylor California rosé" is a funny line: in actuality, Taylor rosé is an inexpensive New York state wine. Since real-life Allen is known to regard anything Californian with disdain, the line from Tom's dream suggests Dream Woody was mocking California by saying this was one of their distinguished wines.

The vagrant and the middle-aged lady out on a walk to kill time represent ordinary people who, in Tom's dream, are not appropriately appreciative of Dream Woody's humor. Tom sees himself as special in being the one who knows to respond to Dream Woody. But then Tom fails at responding because he just didn't get the punch line of Dream Woody's joke. Tom's dream seems to be about his fear that he won't live up to Woody Allen's expectations. He still feels ashamed that he "let that poor guy down," rather than risk a possible admission of his own ignorance, and hopes to have a chance to make it up to Woody, either in a future dream or in his waking life.

Romance and Womanizing

Most of the women I interviewed dreamed of Woody Allen as an object of their romantic and/or sexual desires. In the dreams that follow, the women meet Dream Woody in a variety of situations: on a yellow school bus, in a grocery store, on a baseball field on Fire Island, at a car show, on a green, peaceful island and at a Chock Full o' Nuts among other places. Dream Woody is as accessible to his public as is real-life Woody (despite his desire for privacy, Allen is one of the most visible stars in New York City). Once they meet, some of the women develop deep, quiet relationships with Dream Woody while other dreamers enjoy mutually lustful experiences with him. Still others are disillusioned by the man of their dreams.

What do waking women see in Woody Allen? Allen is wise, witty, athletic, thoughtful, sexy, sensuous, multitalented, creative and highly intelligent.

"God knows what you must think about me," Ike says to Mary their first time alone together, in *Manhattan*. "I think you're fine. Are you kidding?" she answers. "I mean, you do have a—a tendency to get a little hostile, but I find that attractive." Of course, there are countless other qualities that draw women to Allen—and those are reflected in the women's dreams about the artist.

Quiet and Meaningful

•

JOY MAHANES is a forty-year-old counselor in a holistic health-care center. Joy saw Woody Allen in real life once on Fourteenth Street in Manhattan. "He'd disguised himself by wearing no glasses. His hair was longer than usual at the time, too. He was carrying two huge paper bags that looked like they must contain something like pillows. I guess he bought something from one of those cheap, Fourteenth Street stores. I slowed down and smiled as I walked by him, but I didn't speak because I figured he didn't want attention. He smiled, rather embarrassed but sweet, and squinted his eyes at me; he obviously couldn't see well." Joy has seen all of Allen's films, several times each, and says she relates especially to the serious issues Allen deals with: "loyalty, integrity and fear of dying." The following dream from early summer 1978 is one of Joy's many dreams about Allen.

―――――――――――――― **SOUP'S ON** ――――――――――――――

It was the beginning of summer in New York City. I had just moved into an apartment with Diane Keaton. We had been referred to each other by a roommate referral service. I was studying to be an actress, taking a summer workshop at a studio in Greenwich Village. And Diane Keaton was working on a summer production of a stage play.

Diane and I became friends quickly, which I was certainly happy about. Still, at first, I felt somewhat insecure with her, afraid our friendship wouldn't last. But, as the summer went on, my insecurity about her left, and I knew for sure that we were good friends. I remember thinking how great it was to have someone so stimulating and nonpetty for a friend—someone I didn't have to handle with kid gloves.

One afternoon Diane came home early from rehearsal. I was in the bathroom, washing out some things in the sink.

"Guess what! Woody's coming home next week!" she shouted through the bathroom door. I had never heard her sound so happy.

"That's great," I answered, but really I felt a stab of anxiety in my chest, because I imagined this news meant that I would have to move out.

I came out of the bathroom and greeted Diane in person.

"I guess I'd better start looking for another place to live," I said, trying to sound matter-of-fact about it.

"What? Oh, no!" Diane exclaimed. "You can stay here. Woody's really looking forward to sleeping with the two of us; he mentioned that in his letter."

I was thrilled. In the days that followed, I became alternately anxious and confident as I looked forward to Woody's arrival.

Woody moved in with us the next week, just as planned. I was slightly in awe of Woody, but other than that feeling which never really left, I felt at ease. Woody helped me to feel at home just as Diane had.

Our life together was easy and idyllic. There were no hassles and no tensions. Our pleasures were simple ones: we cooked and ate together, and we read a lot. Woody was very quiet, more so than either Diane or me. He didn't reach out to me by asking me a lot of questions and trying to get to know me in that way, but he was considerate of me. And he was always good-tempered and easy to be with. I was mainly conscious of his sweetness.

We slept together in a big, lumpy, old-fashioned bed. A scene I remember vividly is the three of us in bed, me in the middle, with our pillows propped up in back of us. And each of us was reading. I was reading *The New Yorker*. And the feeling all around was one of great affection and warmth.

Toward the end of summer Diane had to go to Buffalo for two weeks. It was a business trip related to the play she was working on. The day she left I felt very anxious. I was afraid that Woody wouldn't pay any attention to me now that Diane was away, that our relationship had substance for him only when we were a three-some. My anxiety came to center on the fear that now Woody would eat his dinners out, rather than at home with me.

At the same time that I was so frightened about what would happen with the relationship between Woody and me, I was also a little excited. I felt an excitement because I wondered if maybe Woody did like me as much as I liked him, and if our relationship might therefore become closer now that the two of us would have some time alone together.

I stayed at home all day the day that Diane left. I didn't want to miss any opportunity to be with Woody. I was sitting in a large, black fake-leather armchair in the living room when Woody came home that day. I couldn't see him enter from where I was seated, but I heard him go into the kitchen. At this point both my anxiety and my excitement intensified, but my anxiety was stronger. Because he hadn't even yelled hello or any greeting to me when he came in, I thought I was being rejected.

Now, the next line I'm going to tell you was the closing line of my dream, and it held great significance.

At the end of my dream, Woody walked out of the kitchen, and he smiled really sweetly at me.

"How do you take your soup?" Woody asked me matter-of-factly.

I knew this question meant that he liked me as much as I liked him and that he wanted to share things with me and to be with me. I felt secure in our relationship at last.

Joy's dream mirrors her waking-life insecurity in rela-tionships with both men and women. Dream Woody was, according to Joy, "just as he is in real life. This dream, even more than my others, made the affinity I feel for Woody tangible because it showed what day-to-day life with him would be like." The "easy and idyllic" relationship Joy has with Dream Woody is seen in many of the women's dreams. Joy, like many of the dreamers, expects to get to know Woody Allen one day.

•

LAURIE SWEENEY is an actress who grew up in Montreal and moved to New York in 1978 to pursue a career on the stage. Laurie says that Woody Allen, like her therapist, encourages her to be independent. She admires Allen for playing himself in his films, and not feeling the need to "lavish himself" with additional assets or false qualities in order to be interesting.

Laurie went to an open call for parts in an Allen film but did not get a part, although she did get to see the filmmaker. She remembers dreams two or three times a week, but the only celebrities she has dreamed about are Woody Allen and Paul Newman. The following, from spring 1979, is her first Woody dream.

 **IN GRANDMA'S HOUSE**

Woody and I were alone together in my pretend grandma's kitchen. Her kitchen was the same warm, comfortable place I remember from childhood.

Woody and I sat close together, leaning across the kitchen table, almost touching each other, as we talked intensely. Woody was encouraging me about my career. But he never offered me a job in one of his films. Instead, he told me who I should go see to advance my career. Woody was an example for me of what I wanted to achieve in my work. I could tell, too, that he appreciated my being with him and learning from him, without trying to get something from him—such as a part in his movie.

As we talked, I noticed how he looked, with his pastel button-down shirt and his undershirt showing. Sex became strongly intimated in our conversation and before I knew it we were in bed in this old musty room in Grandma's house.

The comfort Laurie feels with Dream Woody is reinforced by the safe, protective setting of Grandma's house. The domestic atmosphere of this dream is similar to that in Joy Mahanes's and several of the other women's dreams. These dreams recall romantically domestic scenes from Allen's films: Allan Felix and Linda in *Play It Again, Sam*, for example, on their one night of love together when Allan finally realizes that if he will just relax and be himself, a woman he loves can return his feelings—that she won't even mind that he wears days-of-the-week underwear; Alvy in *Annie Hall* protecting Annie from giant spiders in her bathroom, even after he and Annie have broken up; and Ike and Tracy in *Manhattan*, eating and spilling Chinese food in bed and watching old movies on television. The fact that Dream Woody is both lover and adviser to Laurie is also consistent with the characters Allen plays in his movies. These characters—most notably Allan, Alvy, Ike and Sandy—all give advice freely, usually unsolicited, to both the men and women in their lives.

●

RACHEL DAYS is a sociologist who does manpower surveys for a federally funded research institute. Rachel saw Woody Allen in person once, at the screening of *Annie Hall* in Tarrytown, New York. The screening was later parodied by Allen in *Stardust Memories*. Rachel prefers Allen's recent movies to his earlier, funnier ones because they "are more realistic and easier to relate to." She likes Woody Allen because he is "real and clear." Rachel has had seven dreams about Allen, both before and after seeing him in person. The dream below is from early 1980.

_____ **SEARCHING** _____

I went to a dinerlike coffee shop in midtown, on the West Side, near the Port Authority. I took a seat in a booth near the door, and by a window, where I could see out to the street.

I had heard that Woody Allen occasionally came to this diner. He patronized the place because it was an especially nonchic, out-of-the-way joint where the usual customers might not notice him. In fact, the diner was mostly patronized by middle-aged women from the suburbs.

Sure enough, Woody was in the diner this day; I noticed him across the room. I waited eagerly for him to walk by me on his way out, and soon he did.

Woody came strolling by my booth very slowly. He was smoking a cigarette in a funny, ostentatious way. He would look up to the ceiling as he inhaled and then ritualistically turn his head left and right as he exhaled. His smoking was a way of throwing fans off the track. If a fan thought this man might be Woody Allen but wasn't sure, then seeing him smoke would convince them that it certainly wasn't Woody, because everyone knows Woody Allen doesn't smoke!

Woody kept pausing as he moseyed out, turning around and looking in my direction. But I kept looking down instead of looking at him. I didn't want to seem to be aware of his presence because I didn't want him to think I was a groupie.

After he left the diner, I wondered if I had made a mistake in not looking up at him. Also, it occurred to me that Woody might have been looking for me just as I was looking for him!

In the next scene of my dream it was a few days later and I

was on Fire Island. I was in the Pines, which is a gay community there.

I wandered out onto a huge grassy field by an old resort hotel. At the opposite edge of the field from the hotel was a forest. There were men playing baseball in the field. I wandered out into outfield and just stood there. I acted as though I were covering outfield, but really I was just enjoying the tranquillity of the out-of-doors. It was dusk, and it was very quiet, especially considering that there was a game going on.

Then I saw Woody Allen wandering across the field from the old hotel, just as I had done. He was coming in my direction. I watched him in anticipation. He didn't walk directly by me, but he ended up not far behind me. He took a position there as though he, too, were playing outfield. But really he was, like me, just relaxing.

Being in a gay community was a way of throwing fans off the track. If a fan thought this man might be Woody Allen but wasn't sure, then seeing him with a group of gay men would convince them that it certainly wasn't Woody, because everyone knows Woody Allen is straight!

I had then the same amazing feeling that I had had in the diner, namely that Woody was here looking for me just as I was looking for him! I therefore decided to look at him this time.

We began talking in the outfield. It soon grew dark and the baseball game was over, and Woody asked me to have dinner with him. We walked slowly back to the old resort hotel and into a huge high-ceilinged dining room where dinner was being served. The tables were covered with deep-yellow linen cloths, with napkins to match. A waiter smiled sweetly at us. He was Indian and wore a deep-brown waiter's uniform.

As we walked into the dining room, I enjoyed a pleasant fantasy: I imagined that we were going to fall in love. The fantasy was all the more enjoyable because I was optimistic that it was soon to become true. After all, after a lot of wandering around, Woody and I had finally found each other.

Rachel's dream underscores the great lengths Dream Woody will go to in order to avoid being recognized: smoking a cigarette because he knows that contradicts his public image; going to a homosexual beach community where no one (except Rachel) would think to look for him. Several of the men and women I interviewed expressed concern both in their dreams and in their waking lives about not wanting to appear to Woody to be groupies. Rachel's dream exemplifies this ambivalence. On the one hand she seeks Woody out, going to the places she suspects he might go to in order to get away from his fans, places patronized by people unlike either Dream Woody or herself (middle-aged women and gay men), but then she overcompensates by ignoring Dream Woody even when he indicates he's interested in her. And there is another level on which Rachel's dream can be interpreted. She and Dream Woody are both misfits in the places they visit, and their eventual joining can be seen as the union of two alienated individuals.

•

SANDRA PAPPACHRISTAU is a thirty-seven-year-old commercial artist who owns and manages her own gallery. Sandra grew up in a Christian Scientist home in Boston and Pittsburgh, and moved to New York when she was twenty-one. She is the only one of the dreamers who has seen only one Woody Allen movie—*Annie Hall*. Sandra, who is divorced, had always had a hard time trusting men until she had the following dream in 1979.

――――――――――――― **IDYLL** ―――――――――――――

Life in Manhattan was, as always, competitive and fast, and so I decided to get away for a few days. I went to a small green peaceful island. The island was close to Manhattan, but it was worlds apart in atmosphere. There were fields and fields of deep green grass and soft earth beneath it. The weather was balmy. I felt incredibly relaxed.

There were very few people on the island. It almost gave the illusion that I had the island all to myself. I did soon meet one person, though: Woody Allen.

Woody Allen and I fell in love. It must have been almost immediately, because I don't recall any extended courtship. But we were in love, and the next thing I knew, I was pregnant!

I was pregnant by Woody Allen and I felt very good about it. What I remember most is the feeling of mutual trust between Woody and me. I respected him and I knew he respected me. I felt totally at ease and happy.

This was a breakthrough dream for Sandra. She says that she awoke from her dream with a profound sense of well-being and with an insight that has stayed with her ever since. "I trusted Woody Allen in my dream," she thought, "enough to get pregnant by him! He was trustworthy, and there must be other men in my real life who also are trustworthy." The sparsely populated island near Manhattan can be seen as suggesting that Sandra and Dream Woody, like Rachel and Dream Woody in the previous dream, are somewhat alienated persons whose mutual sense of alienation leads them to each other.

•

SUE GREENSTEIN is a thirty-three-year-old psychotherapist who lives in Queens with her husband of nine years. She has met Woody Allen once: at Gage & Tolner's Restaurant in Brooklyn on August 20, 1972. There was a long period when Sue's marriage was on the rocks. During that time she and her husband tried various ways of making their relationship work, including mate swapping and open marriage. But during troubled times, Sue found that her mind most often turned to Woody Allen. She had the following dream in the winter of 1978, a bad period of her marriage.

_____ **LOVE BOAT** _____

It was a black night and I was alone on a small deserted pier somewhere in China. I was waiting for Woody to come and capture me. The situation was simple and perfect. The body of water was calm. There was silence as I waited for Woody, even as he approached, drifting up to my pier in a small raftlike boat. The openness of the boat matched the openness of the setting.

It was all extremely romantic, even the way we were dressed. I was wearing loose-fitting Indian pants, a pale beige—almost white, and Woody was wearing dark clothing and glasses—just like in real life. I could tell he really liked me just as I could tell he really liked me the night in my real life when I met him in a restaurant in Brooklyn.

Woody was pensive, thoughtful and very concerned about me. He also possessed a fatherly manner. And I felt very young, ten years younger than I actually am.

Woody seemed to be the perfect man, just as he is in all of his films. The main thing is that he knows just how women like to be treated. And, in this dream, I was everything that he wanted in a woman: pure and perfect. He just knew exactly what I wanted and I knew just what he wanted, and what we both wanted was to get away from everybody. So that's what we did.

I joined Woody in this open boat and we left the little dock.

Sue's marriage has improved lately, so she's less obsessed with Woody Allen. "My therapist congratulated me recently," Sue said, "because I'm finally letting go of my Woody fixation. I'd been talking about him in therapy for years. . . . But my shrink never minded: she's really into Woody herself."

Sue's dream, like those of several others, is, on one level, about being protected, being rescued. Also, the image of the open boat setting out to sea signifies a search for meaning at its deepest level. And in this regard, Dream Woody can be seen as the magical traveling companion who will help her to find a protector in her own self. Her dream is highly romantic, which is characteristic of liaisons with Dream Woody. Her choice of the word "capture" ("I was waiting for Woody to come and capture me") and her description of Dream Woody as possessing "a fatherly manner" indicates a need in Sue for mastery from him: a need to be taken care of. "Capture" also suggests an erotic experience.

•

LAURIE SWEENEY also joined Dream Woody on a voyage. Laurie, in her earlier dream, had spent a cozy evening in bed with Woody in her grandma's house.

ROUGH WATERS

Woody and I were in a boat on the ocean and there were rough waters.

"I'm scared," Woody said, and I held him and comforted him.

I, in turn, felt warm and secure just because I was with him. "You're so available to me and to my feelings," I told Woody.

Woody's vulnerability and honesty in Laurie's dream are qualities to which both male and female members of Allen's audience respond strongly. Vulnerability seems to be an intrinsic part of Woody Allen's personality and it is always evident, regardless of the film role he's playing. His honest admission of fear in this dream, though, brings to mind the trembling Woody persona of his earlier movies: the terrified bank robber Virgil Starkwell of *Take the Money and Run*, the reluctant revolutionary Fielding Mellish of *Bananas*, and the panic-stricken guy on his first date(s), Allan Felix of *Play It Again, Sam.*

Laurie's sense of mutual protection enabled her to venture further away from home in this dream, where the ocean again symbolizes the unconscious.

•

BARBARA EPSTEIN is an architectural historian who has seen Woody Allen twice at Elaine's, his hangout on Second Avenue in Manhattan. She says that in real life Allen looked emaciated and self-effacing. Yet Barbara, who has been undergoing Jungian analysis, remembers three dreams about Woody Allen, and she says that these are her only dreams in which the male hero is supportive rather than authoritarian. The dream below, Barbara's first about Allen, is from 1978.

_____ **RESCUED** _____

I was standing on the street quarreling with my boyfriend. My boyfriend was a good-looking man in his twenties. He wore a tweed sport jacket and looked as though he would fit well in *Esquire.*

Suddenly Woody appeared. "You have no right to be talking to her like that! She's a wonderful person," Woody told my date.

It seemed extremely important to Woody to let my boyfriend know just how blind he was being—that he wasn't seeing what a worthwhile person I was.

Dream Woody protects Barbara from a troubled relationship, just as he did Sue Greenstein, whom he took safely away on a love boat. Dream Woody's sudden and convenient appearance in Barbara's dream brings to mind Marshall McLuhan's miraculous emergence in *Annie Hall* to help Alvy win an argument. Alvy, standing in line for a movie, turned to the man behind him, who was pontificating pretentiously about Marshall McLuhan. "... You don't know anything about Marshall McLuhan's ... work!" Alvy said, to which the man replied: "... I happen to teach a class at Columbia called 'TV Media and Culture'!" And here McLuhan himself came out from behind a stand-up movie poster. "Tell him," Alvy said. And McLuhan said: "... I heard what you were saying. You—you know nothing of my work. ... How you ever got to teach a course in anything is totally amazing." "Boy, if life were only like this!" Alvy says to the camera.

●

JEAN VEGAS is a waitress and childcare worker who has lived in New York for six years. She is "intrigued by Woody because he's so intelligent and moody ... and he surrounds himself with beautiful women." Jean's favorite Allen film is *Interiors*. Her dream is from early 1979.

_____ BUT I REALLY COULDN'T SING _____

I dreamed I was Woody Allen's girlfriend, and he wanted me to be in movies.

We were in a studio where Woody was having a discussion with a producer. I remember cameras and a yellow-and-brown couch in the center of the room. Woody told the producer that he wanted me to audition for a particular role.

I went to the audition and I was asked to sing. I couldn't sing; I really couldn't sing. Woody wasn't there at the time, but when he returned the producer told him: "Look—we can't put her in the leading role as you requested: she can't sing!"

But Woody said determinedly, "Well, we'll have to put her somewhere. I really want her to be in this movie.'

I interrupted: "No, it's all right. Please don't worry about it. I'm real shy, anyway."

I was embarrassed that Woody kept insisting that I be in the movie. I had no experience acting, and I knew I wasn't any good.

But Woody was pushing me to be something because he cared about me. And I just kept saying, over and over, "It's okay; really, I don't want to be in the movie."

Woody cared about me a lot and he was being very sweet to me. I appreciated his caring, but I wished he would back off a little!

Jean says her dream helped her see herself as an attractive woman, "since Woody Allen chose me." The dream is reminiscent both of Alvy in *Annie Hall*, who pushes Annie to take adult education courses, and of Isaac in *Manhattan*, who, similarly, urges Tracy to accept an offer to study acting in London against her will. Were Jean's dream to continue, it would be interesting to see if Dream Woody reneged on his commitment. Both Alvy and Isaac later reversed their opinions out of fear of losing the women. Career-promotion dreams involving Allen are also consistent with his real-life practice of providing his past, current—and future—girlfriends with particularly memorable film roles.

Dream Woody is a good listener. He is willing to be silent and to attend to the person he is with. He understands what the other person is communicating, with or without words. This quietly attending Dream Woody reflects real-life Woody Allen, but not the persona of Woody Allen films. The film characters Allen portrays are generally chatty, often abrasively so. However, his nonverbal communication *is* apparent in his expressiveness as an actor. Allen's facial expressions change rapidly and dramatically with a nakedness that often takes us far beyond his words, sometimes even beyond the sense of the script. Consider, for example, Sandy's anguished expressions (in *Stardust Memories*) as he suddenly becomes fixated on the rabbit his cook is preparing for dinner. And *Bananas* has several extended silent cameos of Allen's nonverbal expressiveness: the fear Fielding manifests in his encounter with subway thugs; the erotic eating scene (a parody of the one in *Tom Jones*); and his deep pain while listening to his ex-girlfriend, who does not recognize him disguised as the president of San Marcos, describing how inadequate he was to their relationship.

•

SONIA JACOBS is a television producer who has never met Woody Allen but has seen him many times at Elaine's. The first time she saw him Sonia was on her way to the rest room, and she was so flustered she walked into the men's room. She had a mishap the second time she saw Allen too. She was lighting a match when she glanced up and saw him at a nearby table. Startled, she flipped her match. "The end of the match made a perfect arc, went flying off the match and landed on Christopher Plummer's shirt and set him on fire." Sonia says she had "real eye contact" with Allen on both of these occasions.

Sonia thinks of herself as being very spontaneous and regrets that Woody Allen seems to be repressed in his personal life. She has been in Jungian analysis and has been keeping a dream journal since she was sixteen. She remembers dreams almost every night. She had the following dream on September 29, 1979, the day after her fifth wedding anniversary.

LONG AND LANKY

Woody Allen came to see me at my parents' house. I had a great time showing him all around the house, describing all the things and explaining my life to him.

In spite of the fact that I was self-conscious, I was able to make perfect sense as I explained myself to Woody. And I felt he understood my own peculiar way of telling a story and that, in fact, I came across well.

I was drawn to Woody. And I considered the possibility that, because he is both a director and someone who understood me so well, he could do a good job of portraying the story of my life.

My parents were observing my interaction with Woody. They were fascinated by, and did not understand, the rapport between the two of us. Woody and I were on a different psychic level from my parents.

Woody appeared long and lanky in the legs. He was wearing those baggy khaki trousers that artists wore in the fifties. I noted that they were like the trousers my father-in-law wore in one of the few photographs we have of him.

Throughout my time with Woody I felt that our real communication took place on a nonverbal level. I made sometimes superficial conversation with him while showing him my parents' house. But always, on a deeper level, there was a complete rapport that did not need to be verbalized.

Sonia's dream, on the day after her fifth wedding anniversary, seems to be a symbolic reenactment of the time when she was first getting to know her husband, with Dream Woody acting as a stand-in for her husband. Showing Dream Woody her parents' house was her way of revealing her origins to him. Sonia's dream seems to represent her need to reaffirm the sense that she has complete rapport with someone "on a different psychic level from my parents." Her dream also reveals that it is important to her that her parents see just how different her level of communication with Dream Woody is from her interaction with them. She may have unconsciously chosen Woody to substitute for her husband because, in addition to being a person she respects, Woody is a well-known, indisputably successful man. Sonia's dream seems to represent a struggle to convince herself that her marriage is all that she wants it to be.

•

MIMI JEROME is a harpist. She practices six hours a day and performs on a free-lance basis. When Mimi dreams about her friends she thinks that "they're really in my dreams. . . .

They've come over in real life and they're acting out." She also feels that way when she dreams about Woody Allen. Mimi went to see Allen play the clarinet at Michael's Pub a few months after her first dream about him. Though many of his fans approach him to talk or get autographs during intermission, Mimi was afraid to speak to him for fear that he wouldn't remember her from the dream.

Mimi respects Allen "for being immersed in the world, and for his honesty, which so often goes right to the core of things." She also identifies with his admiration of Ingmar Bergman. The following dream, from December 14, 1979, is Mimi's first Woody dream.

LIKE HARPO

A composer I know asked me to play the harp in an ensemble at Woody's house. Woody had invited Sal, my composer friend, to be a guest at his party, and it was Sal's idea to have me play the harp there.

I got a ride to the party with some other people who knew Woody. And it turned out that Woody rode in the same car as us!

We had to cross the Brooklyn Bridge en route to Woody's house. I had never before experienced the Brooklyn Bridge as being so long. It seemed frighteningly long.

I was afraid of falling. I said: "Look, the bridge sags in the middle!" But no one paid much attention to my fears.

Woody and I barely talked in the car. I felt there was a deliberate evasion going on—a contrived avoidance. Still, after the party, Woody volunteered to take me home.

Woody drove me home to Teaneck in a boat. On the way home I tried to be funny, and I was pretty successful at it, but Woody didn't say much.

At one point, as we were zipping along in the boat, Woody said to me, "Shall I drive you home now?"

I said, "No, it's too early!"

"Oh?" Woody said.

I was embarrassed, but still I felt wonderful about saying to this man: "No, don't take me home; it's too early!" So I said it again: "It's too early!"

Then Woody, with a great intensity, put his hand around my head, pulled me against him and said, "Well, we haven't spoken much tonight."

"It was good not talking to you," I replied.

Mimi's fear about crossing the Brooklyn Bridge is reminiscent of Max Bernstein's fear of accompanying Dream Woody on a cable car across the Harlem River Bridge. In both dreams Dream Woody was stoic about the crossings. And Mimi's return trip with him in a boat is another frequent symbol in this collection of dreams. Crossing a bridge generally symbolizes making a connection between two worlds, and boat trips represent exploration of the unconscious. The ambiguity about detail in the dream (whether the boat was driven on water or land) points, perhaps, to ambivalence in Mimi's feelings. She's also ambivalent about Dream Woody's quietness. Initially she imagines that his silence represents a deliberate evasion, but by the end of her dream she's enjoying the "not talking." Her ambivalence seems to be about trusting Dream Woody. At first she's cynical, but as the dream progresses she begins to trust him so much that she wants the date to continue. "It was good not talking to you" was her lighthearted way of referring to their lack of verbal communication. The absence of conversation in Mimi's dream was eventually experienced as a treat.

•

VERONICA McGUIRE is an art student working her way through school as a typesetter. Veronica hadn't spent much time thinking about Woody Allen until she dreamed about him. She always considered him to be an extremely gifted, multitalented artist, but since her dream, from the summer of 1978, she has felt a personal bond to the artist.

KINSHIP WITH MOON DEER

My friends and I wanted to have a picnic on the moon. And I was delegated to go get permission from NASA for our party. Apprehensively, I went to the agency.

"Oh, yes, the moon is such a lovely place," the woman behind the counter told me. "We've had so many requests from people wanting to go up and explore."

I relaxed and smiled.

"But . . . I'm afraid the moon deer who inhabit the moon don't like people very much at all. It's not that they're hostile; they're just very shy. You'd have to get permission from them."

I sighed.

"There's another catch," the woman went on. "The only human being the moon deer will talk to is Woody Allen! So it's up to you to get Woody Allen to make your request to the inhabitants of the moon. This is your only option. If the moon deer agree you can have your picnic with NASA's blessing!"

I left NASA in a fuddle. "How can deer express themselves?" I wondered.

I got hold of Woody Allen, who was initially reluctant to discuss the matter.

"Please go away," he begged me. "I don't have time for this nonsense."

But I finally convinced Woody that since he was the only human . . .

We arrived on the moon. Woody had a tape recorder slung over his shoulder and a microphone in his hand. The elder of the moon deer came forth to speak to us. The others stood at a distance.

Most of Evelyn's dreams are "a mishmash of Technicolor scenes in which [she is] constantly the loser." So she experienced great relief with this dream, "in beautiful black and white," wherein she finds a soul mate. The most recent Allen film Evelyn had seen before her dream was *Manhattan*, and she had marveled at its black-and-white splendor. So the black and white of her dream served to underscore the idea that this was a unique and important dream and that it was a Woody dream. The collage coming to life in Evelyn's dream is reminiscent of Stephen Wohl's dream in which the movie he was watching came to life and, like Evelyn, he was suddenly transported from L.A. into a New York City street scene complete with Woody Allen. These magical transformations also bring to mind Allen's short story, "The Kugelmass Episode," where Kugelmass, through the aid of the Great Persky and his magic cabinet, can be projected into the novel of his choice. (And, as Persky explains to the initially skeptical Kugelmass, "Not just a novel, either. A short story, a play, a poem.")

Evelyn said that her dream, which begins with her on the outside looking in and ends with her making contact with Dream Woody, reinforced her motivation to become more her own person, as well, of course, as her desire to meet Woody Allen. Her identification with Allen, sharpened in her awareness by the dream, gives her the support she is missing from her friends and family, support that pushes her to be more independent and to take risks.

Toward the end of *Manhattan*, Ike is visiting with Emily (Anne Byrne), whose husband has left her to live with the woman Ike was previously living with. "You seeing anybody?" Emily asks Ike, to which he replies: "Uh, uh, y-you-you know, I-I n-n-never had any problem meeting women." Dream Woody doesn't have any problems meeting women

The moon deer were uncommonly beautiful. They were small deer with long tufted ears and tails like lions. They were delicate creatures.

The moon deer were all intelligent, very sensitive and extremely wise. You could understand them perfectly as they communicated even though their mouths didn't move and they made no sounds.

The elder moon deer was wearing glasses. He and Woody Allen had a brief but meaningful exchange. And we got the permission for our picnic.

This enchanting dream of idealized nonverbal communication captures the essence of Woody Allen's uniqueness. Dream Woody's kinship with the moon deer is emphasized by his close resemblance to them. Like real-life Woody, the deer are small, intelligent, sensitive and wise. Moreover, they "don't like people very much. It's not that they're hostile; they're just very shy." The elder moon deer, presumably the wisest one of all, was even wearing glasses.

In this dream Woody Allen appears to be a link between the physical world, represented by the earth, and the spirit world, represented by the moon and moon deer. The image of a human relating to animals always suggests a spiritual connection. And lunar symbolism is often concerned with death as the first condition of mystical regeneration. The moon's periodic disappearance and subsequent reappearance represents spiritual rebirth. Since Allen is obsessed with death, the moon is a particularly appropriate setting for demonstrating his role in this dream as a link between the two worlds.

•

APRIL AUGUSTINIAK is a twenty-nine-year-old film editor who moved from Ohio to New York in 1974 in order to be near Woody Allen. April comes closer than any other dreamer to fitting the stereotype of a groupie. She has seen her idol many times in many places because her main pastime is following him around Manhattan. In fact, she's become so expert at locating the artist around town that Ron Galella, the notorious paparazzo, asked her to keep *him* posted on Allen's whereabouts. April especially loves Allen's *New Yorker* stories, and although she refuses to pick a favorite Allen movie, she concedes, "*Interiors* is way up there." She denies she's a groupie, and in one sense perhaps she's not: her goal is not to sleep with Woody but to edit his films.

April has been dreaming about Woody Allen since she was in high school. In spite of the varied sites where she's spotted the artist in waking life, most of her dreams are limited to one location, the sculpture garden of the Museum of Modern Art in Manhattan. She's had the dream below many times.

MOMA

It was very dark. The fountains were lit. Everything was stark. There were one thousand extras. I was watching Woody Allen shoot a film in the sculpture garden.

He looked at me and I looked back. And he maintained the eye contact. I was embarrassed, but mostly overjoyed. He looked curious. He looked interested.

Several women who've encountered real-life Allen mention his looking at them with an unflinching gaze. This contrasts with the filmmaker's manner when being introduced to someone, professionally or socially, when he is often too self-conscious to look the person in the eyes.

•

EVELYN MURPHY is a fifty-nine-year-old jazz aficionado and Mensa member who grew up in a Baptist family in Mis-

souri. Evelyn thinks of herself as a survivor. "I l matic childhood and I've long been aware of th laughter as healing." She thinks of Woody Allen a strong person . . . a person who dares to be himse. does not kowtow to the crowd and the mores of so says she has always been inhibited, "feeling that I like other people for the sake of my family, or n band, or my children. . . . I was brought up with will the neighbors say' attitude, and keeping to th not expressing what was in my gut, what was there to be expressed." Evelyn remembers dreams only o few months. The dream below is from 1980.

SOUL MATE

I was looking at a black-and-white collage. It was about tw by thirty, and in the lower right corner was a picture c Allen. His face seemed to be looking right at me, gazing of the frame. As I looked more closely at the collage, I s included other pictures as well. One was of a young wor long dark hair. I thought it might be Ali McGraw, but now met you [the author], I think the picture may have been began to study the collage to see if I could recognize anyo

The next thing I knew I was walking along a street York City! It was night and the whole world was in beautif and white.

Near a corner I stopped and looked across the street. had just stepped up onto the curb. He continued striding very purposefully. I knew he was on his way to jam.

As he strode along, Woody turned around and looke his left shoulder. He caught my eye, and there was, for each a moment of acute awareness of the other's gaze.

Although I had gone to bed feeling lonely, I woke up kn that there was someone I could really identify with. I felt that found a soul mate.

either. Meeting him usually involves an immediate, mutual affinity, the nature of which sometimes seems to exceed the dreamer's best expectations.

●

LIBBY HENDRICKS grew up in St. Louis and, in 1978, moved to New York where she manages a Soho music gallery. Libby enjoys little things: little rooms, little cars, and little men. The dream below is from the fall of 1978.

_____ **ONE GIANT STEP** _____

I was walking around at a car show when who should I run into but Woody Allen! As we looked into each other's eyes we felt an immediate attraction. It wasn't love and it wasn't sex. It was an incredible magnetic attraction.

Woody and I squeezed together into a miniature futuristic sports car-truck. I was in the driver's seat, of course. I started the car.

We drove the car all around the showroom. And as we drove we had an animated and wonderful conversation. We agreed on everything. Mainly Woody and I took turns sharing our experiences with weird people. We both had a lot of these.

We drove our miniature sports car-truck right through the showroom door and out onto a red-brick sidewalk. I felt totally secure with this man.

I knew I'd finally met someone who was an extension of myself: Woody was the person I would be if I could take my brain one step forward.

Libby's matter-of-fact acknowledgment that she "of course" was driving is a detail consistent with both real-life Woody and the characters he portrays in his films, none of whom are fond of driving. "I got, uh, I got a license but I have too much hostility," Alvy explains to Annie in *Annie Hall.*

If the car is thought of as a phallic symbol, then Libby's driving could suggest that she experiences herself as being in control sexually of her relationship with Dream Woody. And that could explain why she felt so totally secure with him.

Libby's summation of Dream Woody as "the person I would be if I could take my brain one step forward" echoes the feelings—and frustrations—of many men and women who identify with the artist.

•

MEREDITH BAUMAN is a lawyer who thinks Woody Allen is bizarre, absurd and fascinating. Meredith has seen him several times, in Elaine's, at Michael's Pub, at Zabar's— the Upper West Side gourmet store—and leaving his therapist's office. The dream below, Meredith's second, is from 1980.

—————————— **VIRGIN BIRTH** ——————————

It was winter and I was lost in the country. I stopped at the first house I saw and rang the doorbell.

Woody Allen opened the door.

"Excuse me. I'm lost. I need to call somebody to come and pick me up."

"Surely, no problem at all," Woody said, indicating the telephone in the kitchen.

I placed my call and found out that someone could come and pick me up in about one hour. I hung up the receiver and picked up a manuscript I had noticed lying on the kitchen counter.

I read a little of the manuscript and then I offered Woody my feedback on what I was reading. Before I knew what was happening, the two of us were collaborating on a magnificent master-piece!

Our affinity for each other was so great that we experienced it as a spiritual connection. It was more than just falling in love.

But Woody brought us briefly back to earth when he announced that he wanted children. I explained to him that I simply did not want to get pregnant and carry a child. I was, however, willing to have children as long as I didn't have to carry them.

"But I have an idea!" I told Woody. "Do you have any meat in your refrigerator?"

I found several pieces of meat in Woody's fridge. I took them and quickly sprouted them in water as though they were plants. And sure enough, little babies—human babies—sprouted from the water.

The doorbell rang. The hour was up and my ride had arrived. I left Woody to decide what to do with the babies.

As we've seen, Meredith's apparently transcendental lust recurs frequently in women's dreams about Woody Allen. The babies, sprouted from meat in water, reinforce the theme of Meredith's extraordinary connection with Dream Woody. The water symbolizes the unconscious as the source of life and the meat can be seen as representing physical life. It was only by placing the meat in water (submerging the physical in the unconscious) that Meredith and Dream Woody's babies were produced.

Meredith's dream also depicts someone overwhelmed by her own creative energy. She has access to her creative imagination and she produces, but she has difficulty persevering. She isn't sure what she wants. While not all women are as nonchalant as Meredith was in leaving Dream Woody with babies after only an hour, almost all relationships with Dream Woody are temporary. This pattern mirrors both real-life Allen, who has a history of brief affairs prior to his relationship with Mia Farrow, and the characters Allen plays in his films, none of whom settle into a lasting relationship. As Ike sighingly says to Mary in *Manhattan*, "Uh, I—I was just thinking there must be something wrong with me because I've never had a relationship with a woman that's lasted longer than the one between Hitler and Eva Braun." The most explicit statement of transience is seen in Mark Goodman's dream.

●

MARK GOODMAN is a certified public accountant who says he receives communications from extraterrestrial beings and, three times, has had premonitions of events that later occurred. He actually looks forward to entering a dream state, and remembers dreams every night. "I will put myself into this dream state at ten o'clock every night seven days a week for the rest of my life," he told me. Mark thinks the following dream anticipates the life-style Woody Allen may choose after he retires from show business. His dream is from the spring of 1980.

WOODY RETIRES

We were north of the Catskills, somewhere in the mountains this side of Canada. I could see Woody Allen. He was sitting in a yellow bus, like a school bus converted into a van.

The bus was parked not far away from a house in the woods. The area was scenic and quiet. Although it was late November, the snow on the ground was surprisingly light.

Woody wasn't going to make any more movies or write any more books. He had fallen into a way of life that satisfied him—a life that was green and peaceful.

Diane Keaton was nearby. She was the one connection with the past that Woody was keeping. Diane, of course, intended to keep her sometimes platonic relationship with Woody on a semicommitted basis, while also having relationships with many other men.

As I watched Woody alone in his bus, I sensed he was inviting me to come in. He is not the type of person who would invite me or anyone to come into his life forever. But I felt he was signaling me to come into the bus and pass some time with him, to share perhaps some words and dreams.

"Nothing can be permanent" was the overriding theme of my dream. Both Woody and Diane knew this.

The romantic Woody Allen of women's dreams is the Allan Felix of *Play it Again, Sam* who buys his best friend's wife the tiny plastic skunk for her birthday that she treasures to an extent that baffles her more prosaic husband, the Alvy Singer of *Annie Hall* who tells Annie: ". . . love is, uh, is too weak a word for what—I . . . I lerve you. You know I lo-ove you, I—I loff you. There are two fs. I-I have to invent— Of course I love you," and to a lesser extent, the Isaac Davis of *Manhattan* who fulfills Tracy's wish for how to spend the evening by taking her on a horse-and-buggy ride through Central Park. The romantic Woody is also the real-life Woody, as his public knows him through published interviews and through empathy with the man behind the persona in his movies, who is quiet, serious, values meaningful relationships and who has longed, often without optimism, for the perfect lifelong mate. In Allen's story "The Lunatic's Tale," Dr. Ossip Parkis asks: "Did anyone I know have a 'meaningful relationship'? My parents stayed together forty years, but that was out of spite." In an interview with Richard Schickel for *Time* in 1979, Allen said, "I've had friends who when they marry say: 'I know we're going to have to work at it.' I always think they're wrong. The things that are really pleasureable to life . . . really require no effort." And in an interview with Frank Rich in the same issue of *Time,* Allen said: "I'm against the concept of short marriages, and regard my own marriages as a sign of failure. . . ."

Later, Richard Corliss wrote in *Film Comment:* "It's a mark of growing up that *Annie Hall* and *Manhattan* define a serious search for something the young Woody only joked about: an enduring relationship." Still, as recently as *Stardust Memories*, that search seems to be one that befuddles and torments Allen. As Sandy Bates, the famous filmmaker who has a history of being attracted to neurotic women, Allen decides at the conclusion of *Stardust* to pursue a relationship with Isobel, who is supposed to represent a mature choice for a mate. But Sandy's expression of commitment to her is so cute it's hard to take seriously. And although Isobel is less neurotic than the two other women in Sandy's life, she is not impressively mature. She is so narcissistic that she does isometric exercises to tone her facial muscles while Sandy is earnestly trying to discuss the future of their relationship. When Sandy complains that her facial contortions are distracting and that what he is talking about is important, Isobel inanely replies: "Yes"—motioning to her distorted face— "but my exercise, too!" The character of Isobel seems to fit more a superficial stereotype of maturity: she is buxom and has children. In his search for an enduring relationship, Alvy Singer showed more insight at the end of *Annie Hall,* I think, than Sandy Bates did at the end of *Stardust Memories.*

The rewards of an enduring relationship are perhaps most strongly emphasized in *Zelig,* in which Leonard Zelig is cured by, and subsequently marries, Dr. Eudora Fletcher (Mia Farrow). The cure and union led "Scott Fitzgerald" to write: "In the end it was, after all, not the approbation of many but the love of one woman that changed his life."

The search for a lasting relationship is also reflected in the women's dreams about Woody. And the romantic version of Dream Woody is certainly endowed with several of the characteristics that usually make for enduring relationships (respectfulness, attentiveness, excellent communication). Still, as a group, the women's dreams about Allen suggest they sense a transience about him. It is striking that not one woman referred to her relationship with Dream Woody as a permanent one. Not one woman dreamed that she was married to or planning to marry Woody. The dreamer and Woody were often soul mates as well as bedmates, but they never took vows of lifelong bliss. Toward the end of *Annie Hall*, bewildered as to how his relationship with Annie failed, Alvy stops an older woman on the street to get her opinion on what he might have done wrong. "Never something you do," she says. "That's how people are. Love fades."

In contrast to the romantic version of Dream Woody, there is also a kinky Woody who appears in dreams. These sexy dreams capture the spirit if not the actual character of real-life Woody Allen. In a 1980 interview with Tony Schwartz for *The New York Times*, Allen's close friend Tony Roberts said: "Put it this way, Harpo Marx probably chased the most girls. I chase the second most and Woody is a close third." In the dreams that follow, Woody doesn't have to chase too hard.

Kinky

•

DEBORAH DUANES is a thirty-six-year-old medical abstractor who likes Woody Allen because he seems uniquely perceptive. Her nocturnal visions of Allen, seven to date, began after her waking-life subway encounter with him. She had the following dream on a hot summer night in 1980.

ORAL SEX

I was riding in a yellow bus, like a school bus, and I was in Atlanta. The bus was transporting people home from an outdoor concert that had been held in an outlying area of Atlanta.

Woody Allen had the seat in back of me on the bus. There was no one seated next to either of us. He initiated a conversation and shortly afterward moved up to sit next to me. His moving up to sit beside me meant that we were now on a date.

We arrived at the house where I was living while in Atlanta. There was a wonderful veranda with one of those old porch couches that swing back and forth when you sit on them. And there were huge lilac trees and magnolia bushes around the veranda. It was late at night, and it was humid. The air was heavy with the aroma of lilacs and magnolias. It was very romantic. It made me think of Faulkner and Tennessee Williams.

Woody lay down on the couch and then he pulled me on top of him. I was lying on top of him, and he gently pulled my head toward his, and then began to kiss me. It was nice at first: the kisses were warm.

Then, something extraordinary happened: as we were kissing, Woody began to ejaculate from his mouth. He was ejaculating from his mouth into mine, and I thought, ''Well, Woody Allen really *is* different!'' I didn't want to swallow the semen, but, on the other hand, I didn't want to hurt his feelings. So, I did, in fact, swallow his semen.

After Woody finished coming, I raised my head back just a little way to look into his face. Here I experienced another surprise, for: much to my amazement, Woody's face had turned into Marlon Brando's!

As in so many of the dreams, Dream Woody again manages to do the unexpected—in this case, the extraordinary. While

Deborah was surprised, her response seems rather low-key. She notes that Dream Woody's feat confirms his uniqueness but then her thoughts immediately go to the relatively pedestrian considerations some women have when performing ordinary fellatio. In discussing her dream, Deborah said the main feeling she had was of extreme intimacy with Woody. Dream Woody's ejaculating from his mouth while they were kissing was, perhaps, a way of denoting the exceptional intimacy of those kisses. Dream Woody's subsequent transformation into Marlon Brando brings to mind the image of Brando as he appeared in *Last Tango in Paris,* in which he portrays a very raunchy, kinky lover. Deborah's dream seems to be a comment on Dream Woody's perversion by saying that it seems more like something Brando would do.

Real-life Woody Allen may not be quite as "different" as Deborah's Dream Woody, but her waking-life experience with him in a subway station is typical of real-life Allen. In a 1975 interview at the New School for Social Research, Allen said that "girl chasing"—roaming the streets of Manhattan and the trails of Central Park—was one of his favorite pastimes. He also said that his celebrityhood helped him in picking up women only in that they knew he wasn't a rapist or a maniac. But he still got "a lot of no's." Deborah Duanes regretted her real-life no to Allen. According to Deborah, when she looked up and saw that she had just turned down a date with Woody Allen, she froze, made speechless by the realization. Allen, meanwhile "turned immediately and began walking away from me with tiny but extremely fast steps. He was up the staircase and gone from sight by the time I caught my breath."

•

ANN BERLIN is a word processor and an active NOW member who adores New York and "wouldn't leave at gunpoint." Ann, who is twenty-six, thinks of herself as "the world's oldest college junior." She's had lots of dreams about Woody Allen, but the one below is her "epic Woody dream." Ann moved to New York from Memphis two weeks after having had this dream in June 1979.

THE SCRABBLE GAME

I was in a very small grocery store with wooden floors. I was new to New York. The prices in this store were very high. They had mostly gourmet food. I stopped pushing my grocery cart and picked up a can of black olives to see if they had pits in them or not. After reading the label, I turned to put the can in my basket, which was empty. As I turned around, I saw that across the aisle from me was Woody Allen. He also had a shopping cart with nothing in it, and he was looking at a label.

I gathered up all my charm and said "Hello." Woody was wearing a green T-shirt that was tie-dyed and very old. Over it he had on a work shirt and old blue jeans and white sneakers. His hair was all messed up. "Would you like to have coffee with me?" he asked.

"Well, I guess so; I don't have anything in my basket here," I answered. I quickly put my olives back on the shelf. Then, since neither of us had anything in our shopping carts, we just left them standing in the aisle, and we left the store together.

"Why did you come to New York?" Woody asked me as soon as we were outside.

I decided to tell him the truth. "Well, fifty percent of the reason I came to New York is you, and the other fifty percent is Al Pacino." He looked at me with disbelief.

"Do you play Scrabble?" he said.

"As a matter of fact, I've never been beaten," I told him.

Woody became very excited. "I could just tell from talking to you that you were a Scrabble player!" he exclaimed. "Would you play Scrabble with me right now?"

"I don't know. What time is it?" I asked.

He looked at his Mickey Mouse watch. "Four-thirty," he told me.

"I guess it's okay if we play Scrabble," I said calmly.

We walked along the city streets at a fast pace. Woody was eager to get me to his Scrabble board. But on the way a window display of a French bakery caught Woody's attention.

"I have to stop for a chocolate éclair," Woody said, out of the blue. "Do you want anything?"

"No, I'll just wait out here," I replied, thinking of my weight.

Woody rushed into the bakery. When he reappeared he was finishing off a chocolate éclair.

"There," he said, with a gratified sigh.

Soon we arrived at an elegant apartment building with an awning and a doorman. "Hello, Mr. Allen," the doorman said. "Hello, Fred—hello, Fred," Woody said, somewhat gruffly. The lobby of this building was so elegant Woody looked funny in it.

A maid opened the door to Woody's apartment. She had red hair and a little apron just like Hazel. Woody was very businesslike with the maid. "I want you to set up the Scrabble set on the terrace and I want you to do it right now," he ordered her. "Bring the dictionary and paper and pencil," he said rapidly. "Yes, sir—yes, sir," she responded.

We went through long sliding glass doors onto a beautiful terrace with wrought-iron work and wrought-iron chairs. The maid set everything up for our game. Woody had Scrabble Deluxe with a turntable, and he had a big, high-quality dictionary.

The maid was hovering over the table. "Will there be anything else?" she asked. "Yes, I want this made very clear," he said, emphatically. "While we are playing Scrabble, Maria, I do not want to be disturbed. I don't care who it is. I do not want to be disturbed."

The Scrabble game went very fast. Right at the beginning I made up my mind to let him win. The game in this dream was not true to reality, because in Scrabble, you can only make words of seven letters. But in my dream game most of the words Woody made were longer than seven letters. And every word he made was obscene or sex-related.

Woody spelled the words "cunnilingus," "fellatio," "sodomy" and "masturbation." Each time he made one of these words, he looked at me with a look that said, "Are you going to comment?" But I just acted like it was a normal, ordinary game of Scrabble.

Woody spelled the word "analingus," and with that, the game was over. He won by two points because I let him win. He was very excited about winning. "I won!" he kept repeating. "Great, great!" And I replied demurely, "Yes, you did win, Woody."

Woody then called to Maria the maid. She came outside with a tall stack of phone messages. "All right, who called?" he demanded. The messages mostly pertained to show business. But then Maria got to the last message, which was of more interest to me.

"Mr. Pacino called," Maria read. "He wants to invite you to a party at his estate on Long Island."

Woody turned to me. "Want to go?"

"Me?" I exclaimed. Then I collected myself and added with more poise: "I don't know; what time is the party?"

"Noon," Woody said.

"I suppose I can go. But why are you inviting me?" I had to know the truth; this was all too good to believe.

"There is a reason," Woody admitted. "I want you to meet Al Pacino because I know you'll be disappointed in him. Most women are. He's very short and he lacks my raw animal magnetism. Once you've met Al, then I can become one hundred percent of the reason you're in New York, instead of just fifty percent."

After that Woody walked me home.

This dream, in which cerebral activity possesses an erotic quality ("Woody was eager to get me to his Scrabble board"), brings to mind Allen's short story "The Whore of

Mensa." In the story a man seeks out a private investigator because he's being blackmailed over his relationship with a young woman. He describes the experience to the investigator, Kaiser Lupowitz: "Eighteen years old. A Vassar student. For a price, she'll come over and discuss any subject—Proust, Yeats, anthropology. Exchange of ideas. You see what I'm driving at? . . . I mean, my wife is great, don't get me wrong. But she won't discuss Pound with me. Or Eliot. I didn't know that when I married her. See, I need a woman who's mentally stimulating, Kaiser. And I'm willing to pay for it. I don't want an involvement—I want a quick intellectual experience, then I want the girl to leave. Christ, Kaiser, I'm a happily married man."

In her dream, Ann, who considers herself an active feminist, engages in a rather old-fashioned, sexist ploy: although she's never been beaten at Scrabble, she decides at the outset to let Dream Woody beat her, presumably to bolster his male ego. He won the game after spelling "analingus," and it's tempting to interpret this as Dream Woody's way of saying he knows Ann is brown-nosing him by permitting him to win. Regardless, Ann's Dream Woody is competitive. Already on this first date, he's eager to squelch the appeal his rival, Al Pacino, holds for her.

It's curious that Ann's Dream Woody addressed the doorman as "Fred," the name that, in Fred Forman's dream, Woody reserved for "people I don't know."

•

JASON WEIL'S earlier dreams about Woody Allen had to do with catching up with him artistically, and living the life he lives. In this, his third dream about the artist, Jason gets even closer to Dream Woody.

THE THREE OF US

I was with my big blond girlfriend and I got the one wish of my life: for her and me and Woody Allen to be together in a bed situation. It was hilarious. It was something I've always wanted to do and it was wonderful. I was laughing, Woody was laughing, the girl was laughing. We were in and out of the covers, all crawling around.
It was a real fun night.

The laughter, exuberance and spontaneity in this dream evoke the spirit of sex in Woody Allen's movies. In spite of the anhedonia (a pathological inability to be happy) that Allen says he suffers from in real life, he manages to create numerous joyful moments for his audience. Jason's dream brings to mind a scene in *Sleeper* in which Miles (Allen) and Luna (Diane Keaton) are uninhibitedly frolicking under the covers, with Miles surfacing only occasionally to adjust the boxing glove he's wearing.

•

TOBY DUBREN is a recently divorced photographer who became obsessed with Woody Allen after seeing him at F.A.O. Schwartz, the Fifth Avenue toy store, in real life. She spotted Allen in the store one afternoon just two weeks after moving to New York from Ohio. "He stared at me for around one minute," she said in describing the encounter. Soon after the F.A.O. Schwartz sighting, in the fall of 1978, Toby went to see the object of her obsession at Michael's Pub. That night she had the following dream.

AT FIRST BITE

I was in a beautiful bedroom in one of those enormous beds. The room was a sepia tone, with soft pinks and reds. At first I felt as though I were sleeping. But then I saw a shadow by the window, and it was Dracula! He started to approach my bed. As he came closer, I saw that it was actually Woody Allen in a black Dracula outfit! He was coming closer and closer to me with the intention of biting me on the neck.

Woody had the half-frown, half-smile, quiet look that he has whenever he appears in my dreams. (I remember seeing Woody Allen's face in many dreams. I don't remember the content of those dreams, but I frequently wake up seeing his face, and it's always with this same semisad look, a half-smile, a half-frown and no words. Woody Allen never speaks in any of my dreams.)

Now, as Dracula, Woody had this same semisad expression and he was, of course, silent. Still I could tell that he felt affection for me. I deliberately became very passive, because I have a tendency to talk too much and to dig my own grave in that way.

I waited passively for Woody to bite me. In fact, I couldn't wait for him to bite me! I wanted Woody to bite me so much, but I woke up before he got to.

Once again, Dream Woody was quiet and lustful. Toby says she hopes real-life Woody is the way he was in her erotic dream and as he seemed to be at F.A.O. Schwartz, instead of the way he was at Michael's Pub. At the jazz club, she said, "he seemed like he could not stand those people looking at him."

•

JULIA WELLSLEY is a journalist with a national reputation. Julia has studied music as a serious hobby for several years. Until recently she retained an intense fear from childhood of speaking up in a classroom situation. Her anxiety about being called on in music class was so overwhelming that she considered giving up the hobby rather than to suffer through any more classes. She says her anxiety was intensified by the fact that she viewed her fear as an extreme aberration.

What other competent, successful adult, she asked herself, could be so easily reduced to feeling as vulnerable as a frightened child? Julia found an answer to that question about five years ago when she was privileged to be a guest at one of the rare interviews given by her favorite filmmaker, Woody Allen.

Julia was amazed by the look of real terror on Allen's face as he entered the room and began to answer questions from the audience. It was clear to her that Allen's fear was genuine, and the revelation that a person of his stature could experience anxiety of such intense proportion, in a relatively innocuous situation, brought her tremendous relief. After that she felt less concerned about revealing her own anxiety, and before long she was successful in overcoming her long-standing fear. Her dream is from 1978.

BEARDED WOODY

Woody and I were lovers. He was a sweet and quiet guy, and our relationship was definitely meaningful, but it had a clandestine feel to it. I think that had to do with the air of secrecy Woody had to maintain in order to keep his personal life private.

Woody would sneak to my apartment late each night. My little apartment was on the ground floor and my front door opened up right onto the sidewalk. We may have been in New York, but something about it has always made me think we were in Italy.

Each night I would eagerly open the door and it would always be pitch-black out, and there would be Woody with his wonderful, sad, dark eyes and with the long orange beard he wore to disguise himself.

We'd head right away to my little bedroom, with the bed pushed flush against the wall, and we'd begin making love. Woody was sweet and affectionate and quiet, and our lovemaking was always wonderful.

Sometimes when Woody would arrive late at night, we'd be so hot we'd rush to bed so quickly that he wouldn't have time to take off his beard. And while we were making love his beard would spread over my breasts. And it was soft and warm and furry like a cat.

Julia says that in her dream Woody was like the rabbi in one of Allen's stories, "Hassidic Tales, with a Guide to Their Interpretation by the Noted Scholar," in which there is a Rabbi Raditz of Poland, "a very short rabbi with a long beard, who [oddly enough] was said to have inspired many pogroms with his sense of humor." Julia's bearded Dream Woody also brings to mind Fielding Mellish, dressed as the bearded president of San Marcos, in bed with Nancy (Louise Lasser) in *Bananas.*

•

JENNY SINGER is a stained-glass artist who likes Woody Allen in spite of "his constant searching out of non-Jewish women." She's seen him in person twice, once having lunch in the garden of the Museum of Modern Art in 1974 and then walking along Madison Avenue in 1979. But her one Woody Allen dream dates back to 1971, early in her first marriage.

_____ **ONCE IS QUITE ENOUGH** _____

Woody Allen threw a party a few blocks down from my house on Ocean Avenue in Brooklyn. It was a crowded party, and a lot of my old friends from high school were there—Suzie and Pammy and quite a few of my friends.

After partying awhile, Woody approached me and my two close friends, Suzie and Pammy, and suggested we go into the bedroom and smoke some pot.

Once we were in the dark and dingy bedroom Woody started

acting nervous. He was really afraid his mother was going to come in and catch us smoking. He was obviously scared of his mother and I found it annoying that he was being such a baby.

Pretty soon Suzie and Pammy drifted away. Woody and I were left alone in the bedroom.

We began having sex immediately. I was on top, and the sex was fine. But as soon as we finished having sex I suddenly remembered I was a married woman!

A terrible fear went through my body. Now it was my turn to be afraid of getting caught. I was terrified that Woody would tell my husband, Lionel.

All of a sudden, I saw a way out. There was a knife nearby and I reached for it. I was still on top of Woody and I began to stab him.

I stabbed Woody in the stomach repeatedly, about ten times. And all the while he was making grotesque and horrifying facial expressions.

Woody died. And I walked home alone on Ocean Avenue. The street was empty and I felt an isolation I'd never felt in my whole life.

I woke up in a cold sweat.

Fortunately for Dream Woody, Jenny is the only dreamer who felt guilty about her clandestine affair with him. Jenny says that in her waking life she had not been aware of having sexual feelings for men other than her husband, but after the dream it occurred to her that she felt more than a little trapped by her marriage. Killing Dream Woody was Jenny's attempt to suppress her feelings, but even though he died, her feelings remained to haunt her through the isolation this suppression produced. It's intriguing that it's only after criticizing Dream Woody for being afraid of getting caught misbehaving that Jenny discovers she has the same fear. Perhaps she needed to see her fear in another person before she could recognize it in herself. And of course, Woody Allen is a perfect mirror for anxiety.

•

FARREL DONOVAN is a six-foot-four-and-a-half-inch biographer who thinks Woody Allen is "an important person in the whole history of film. . . . But I'm not struck by his being a great artist or a moralist, I'm struck by his technique. At worst I still think of him as a stand-up comic. I'd like to get him once and tell him, "For Chrissake, stop the one-liners. I mean life is not going to a nightclub." Like several of the male dreamers, Farrel finds himself competing with Allen. His second dream about the filmmaker, from August 1979, posits a surprising theory for Dream Woody's success.

──────────── **NOTEWORTHY** ────────────

I was talking to an attractive young lady, a blonde, who said she was having an affair with Woody Allen. I told her I had heard that Allen engaged in very kinky sex. "Is that true?" I asked.

"No," she said. But I was still curious and I kept firing questions at her. "Well, how is he to have sex with?" I asked.

"Well, he's marvelous," she told me. "Not only that, but he has the largest cock of any man I've ever been with."

"But he's so small!" I said. "How could he have such a large cock?"

"But he does," she kept saying.

"Well, I don't believe you; you're just saying this," I concluded, ready to dismiss the subject.

"Okay," she said. "Okay, I'll bring you a picture." And the next day she brought me a group photograph. There were twenty or thirty friends in an outdoor shot. And everybody in the photo was fully clothed, with the exception of Woody Allen, who was nude.

There was Woody, standing right in the middle of this group of people, and he had a cock that hung down to his knees!

"See!" my friend said triumphantly.

And I thought: "No wonder he's a famous director! No wonder he's a millionaire!"

Jewish Women

"The failure of the country to get behind New York City is—is anti-Semitism," says Alvy to Rob in *Annie Hall*. However, in spite of Allen's frequent expressions of concern about anti-Semitism, *he* is sometimes accused of bigotry because of his alleged adulation of *shiksas*. Several of the Jewish women interviewed for this book were resentful of Allen's apparent preference for gentile women, though they were all ready to forgive him for it.

●

In **ANN WEIDE'S** earlier dream she made a film with Woody in which they played Siamese twins. In the dream below they act in a second film together, and this time Ann gets to be Dream Woody's shrink.

I WAS HIS SHRINK

Woody asked me to do a cameo in a movie in which I would play his therapist. Diane Keaton was also in the movie and naturally she played Woody's goyish girlfriend. The film went like this:

Woody was in therapy with me and he was very antagonistic—threatened by me because I'm a Jewish woman. These personal feelings were keeping him from seeing me realistically as a human being. But it was a mutual thing. I was losing my objectivity as his therapist because I was having personal feelings about him, too. He kept talking about his girlfriend and I was getting—maybe jealous. So I said we should definitely terminate the therapy. "I can recommend some other people for you to go to," I advised him. I was very mature. But then I added that now I might as well tell him what I really think of him. "You should get your act together," I told Woody. "You've been depending on too many other people." I felt rather condescending. I felt like what I really wanted to say was, "Look—calm down! You're highly neurotic!"

We ended the therapy and time went by, and Woody started having problems with his goyish girlfriend, Diane Keaton. One night he saw me out on a date with another man. As he watched me, he suddenly recognized how realistic I am. I was laughing and enjoying myself, and Woody was just suffering.

Woody called me up first thing the next day. "I think we should see each other," he said. That was the end of the movie. Woody didn't end up with Diane Keaton this time: he ended up with me.

And so Ann's wish-fulfillment dream describes the way her ideal Woody Allen movie would turn out—with the Jewish heroine winning out over the WASP.

•

BERYL KOENINGSBERG is a thirty-year-old choreographer who is attracted to Woody Allen but thinks he is "screwed up in his relationships with women." When Beryl was thirteen she wrote Allen and he wrote back. She was an observer in the following dream, which she had in 1978.

PUNKY ROSE

I could see Woody Allen. He was wearing pajamas and he was in his bedroom, a colorful and ornate room. There was a floral bedspread, and appealing low lighting.

Woody was sitting in the middle of his bed, going through a pile of scripts: reading them, studying them carefully.

The phone rang and Woody answered it on the first ring. It was Rose!

Rose is a dancer, a student of mine. She's Jewish and very punky-looking.

From Woody's end of the conversation I could tell that he and Rose were involved in an intense affair. I was quite surprised. First of all, Woody was married, and I wondered how he managed to conduct this affair without his wife finding out.

Even more startling to me, however, was his choice of Rose. Rose has a big nose and is very obviously Jewish-looking. And Woody, of course, generally doesn't like Jewish women.

I was rather excited by this revelation. I figured that if Woody could like a punky Jew like Rose, chances were he could like me, too.

Another happy ending for Jewish women.

Disrespect

Among the women I interviewed, the charge of anti-feminism was made in the same spirit as was the charge of anti-Semitism, with more ambivalence and curiosity than anger. Some of the women just aren't sure where Woody Allen stands, as his work is open to contradictory interpretations on these issues. But there is a running theme through some of these dreams, most—but not all—of them women's dreams, in which Allen is disrespectful to women in a variety of ways, primarily by humiliating them or using them for sex.

These dreams suggest that Allen's treatment of women may be a bigger issue for some of the dreamers than they realize.

•

LYN RUBIN is a Brooklyn artist who thinks Woody Allen is "a real and very sensitive person who is giving the world something." Her dream, from December 1979, anticipated the spirit of *Stardust Memories*.

——————— STARDUST PREMONITIONS ———————

My sister agreed to go with me to try to meet Woody Allen. My sister is a lovely person. She's younger than I am, but people often think she's older because she's taller.

I got real dressed up because I wanted to make an impression.

We went to Woody's apartment building. Amazingly, we didn't have any trouble getting in. The doorman didn't try to stop us.

I knocked on the door of Woody's apartment. He looked through the peephole and called "Who is it?" Of course, he didn't recognize our names. I could feel his apprehension even through the door. Nonetheless, he opened the door and let us in.

Inside Woody's apartment a bunch of guys were sitting at a round table, engaging in a lively conversation. When they saw my sister and me, they fell silent. The men were so polite that they got up and left the apartment. They wanted to give us a chance to talk with Woody.

I didn't know what to say to Woody. I felt intellectually inadequate compared to him. I thought all I could do in this situation was to be nice and attractive.

As neither my sister nor me was saying anything, Woody made some small comments. My sister stood to the side and was nudging me that we should go.

"He knows I don't have anything to say," I thought. And I knew he thought women who didn't have anything to say were nauseating.

Still I wanted to stay just because I wanted to be in his presence. I kept moving closer to Woody though I knew I was being annoying. I touched his arm lightly.

"If you don't stop it and leave me alone, I'm going to throw up on you!" Woody said.

I finally spoke. "Oh, come on," I said. And Woody threw up on me.

"His humor can be very literal at times," I thought. And I indicated to my sister that I was ready to leave now.

My sister and I turned and went back out the door. I felt ashamed of my nauseating behavior.

Lyn's masochistic dream taught her that she needs a sense of purpose and shouldn't think so little of herself. The dream, she says, gave her new insight into Allen, and although she thinks the real-life artist has "more class" than her Dream Woody, she suspects that the contempt portrayed in her dream might have some basis in real life. In Allen's story "Retribution," for example, Harold Cohen, "scrawny, long-nosed, twenty-four-year-old, budding dramatist and whiner," complains, "All the little groupies and secretaries that paraded through the bedroom left me empty; even worse than an evening alone with a good book." In a 1980 interview with Tony Schwartz in *The New York Times* Allen said: "The business I'm in is full of beautiful women, but what good is it if they have nothing to say?" A couple of the women I interviewed recalled being disturbed by this remark. They felt Allen was putting women down. In fact, however, the comment shows his respect for women and his lack of interest in them as mere sex objects. In a scene from *Stardust Memories* celebrity film director Sandy Bates arrives at his hotel room one night to find a girl in his bed. She had tipped the porter to get into his room. She explains that she came all the way from Bridgeport to make it with him. Sandy, astonished, exclaims: "You-you got in a car and you drove a-a-a long distance to go through mechanical sex with a stranger. Is this what you-what you do?" And the girl, Shelly, replies, "Well, my husband drove me. . . . He would be so honored if I could tell him that we made it. He's-he's a-he's a great fan of yours." Sandy, exhausted, pleads with her to leave. "Hey, look, I don't feel that well. I'm tired. I don't want to go through an empty experience." But Shelly has an answer to that, too. "Listen," she says softly, "empty sex is better than no sex, right? Come on, don't be so angry."

•

ESTHER STERN is a typesetter who ran into Woody Allen in real life once, when she was coming out of her therapist's office. Esther thinks Allen keeps himself from being happy for fear that his work will suffer if he is. She likes all his movies, from *What's Up, Tiger Lily?* on, and her favorite is always the most recent film out. The dream below, from 1976, is the first of several she had about the filmmaker.

_____ **MAYBE HE'LL CALL** _____

I was at a party crowded with fashionable, arty people and tinkling glasses. I didn't know any of the other guests, but I did recognize Woody Allen.

Woody started talking to me and we liked each other immediately. So we went to a couch and started necking.

I was enjoying the necking, sexually speaking. But underneath the sexual pleasure was this awful anxiety. I was afraid Woody was going to do something terrible to me. He did.

Woody abruptly let go of me, got up and left. As he was walking away, he called to me that he would return. But I knew I'd been exploited.

The other guests pointed their fingers at me and snickered and guffawed. "You——!" they laughed.

I woke up feeling rotten.

Why did Dream Woody take off? Maybe he experienced a sudden urge for an evening alone with a good book. Or maybe he decided that no sex was better than empty sex after all. Regardless, the incident from Esther's frame of reference is clear: Dream Woody humiliated her.

•

MANNY DEBUC is a child-care teacher who grew up in Mexico and now lives in Los Angeles. Manny, who was in a seminary for three years, thinks Woody Allen is "unusual as an artist because he is honest about feelings, about trying to get in touch with his own feelings." Manny writes his dreams down in the morning, first in Spanish and then in English. The following dream is from September 21, 1979.

—————— FRIDAY MORNING DREAM ——————

Garry Trudeau and another man are playing football on an immense football field full of snakes. I spot them on my walk. I'm walking from the seminary, which is in the middle of a valley, to town. Where I am now the terrain is flat and you can see in the distance that all is farming land and it's a dark brown color. It's just after harvest and the soil is plowed, turned. The sky is dark at the horizon, but where I am it is always light, like stage lighting.

I'm dressed up and I'm uncomfortable because of my shoes and the flesh color of my clothes. I think I am dressed in an unusual way. I'm on my way to the highway to hitchhike or to take a bus to town.

I look now at the giant football field with Garry Trudeau himself, and it is exactly like I've seen it in a comic strip. I go up to

Trudeau and ask him: ''Why in real life do you still look like a cartoon?''

He gives me a scientific explanation. At this point I realize the football field is full of snakes of all shades. I get out of the field immediately and notice that the expanse of the valley is strewn with bright white angular industrial discards. And now it is clear to me that all along Garry Trudeau has really been Woody Allen.

Woody knows I need a ride. ''Go in the house and wait,'' he says. He'll join me shortly and after that give me a ride. But I know the ride won't be to town, where I want to go. I do as he suggests, nonetheless. I had not wanted to go to town that badly.

The house is white, massive, rectangular and has a flat roof like those in vogue in the forties or fifties. The house is bright in contrast to the cloudy, dark background. The house looks west. Inside, the house is big, like the Bonaventure Hotel. It is open and there is a huge fountain like a pond with water jets making monotonous noise.

As soon as I walk in, Woody Allen greets me from the third story, even though I had just left him outside! Woody is reclining on a sofa and I can see his chest is bare. ''Come up,'' he calls and I do. I realize as I ascend the stairs that he's completely naked. I don't see his nakedness; I just sense it. I realize I've made a mistake in climbing up to his level because the people downstairs are upset. They think I'm brazen. They're Woody's fans, and I'm his friend. In spite of their disapproval, I continue talking with Woody Allen.

Woody and I are interrupted by his female companion or wife, Cynthia Anderson, a well-known photographer. She's loud and angry and naked. I *see* her nakedness. Her body is well rounded in the dream, unlike the real Cynthia Anderson, who is very slender. She puts on a robe. Woody is upset and tells her she shouldn't have exposed herself like that in front of me. And now I leave.

While walking down the stairs, I hear that he is beating her.

By the time I get to the first floor, I know she has just had a miscarriage. We all know.

I walk across a shallow path in the fountain. To my left I see the entrance to a gigantic, clean, well-kept sewer. The water is crystal-clear, but it flows up instead of down. I puzzle over this, but don't figure it out.

Manny's strong dream is filled with implications for him. Above all, the dream suggests he is involved in a moral conflict or afraid of pursuing some goal that his unconscious is reminding him of repeatedly. His confusion over what to do, or his resistance to doing so, is summarized by the impossible crystal-clear sewer where the water flows up instead of down.

In the dream Garry Trudeau seems to represent success in a cultured, urban society. When Manny realizes Trudeau is just a cartoon character, Trudeau is transformed into Woody Allen, a stronger symbol perhaps, because he exists in flesh and blood.

It's interesting that this transformation takes place at the moment Manny notices the serpents. The juxtaposition of snakes, very potent mythological symbols of transformation and renewal, with two comic figures, Trudeau and Allen, seems to reflect Manny's desire to deflate the moral issue he is avoiding. Snakes can also symbolize a destructive force, such as the devil or a figure from the underworld. In this case, the snakes might be seen as pointing to the character of Dream Woody that is revealed when he beats his mate, causing her to have a miscarriage. Manny's dream illustrates a struggle to define good and evil, a struggle embodied in a conflict between primitive, ancestral forces and forces of the modern world: on the one hand, there is the football field full of snakes of all shades, and on the other there is the symbol of urban waste—the valley strewn with bright white angular industrial discards.

The moon deer were uncommonly beautiful. They were small deer with long tufted ears and tails like lions. They were delicate creatures.

The moon deer were all intelligent, very sensitive and extremely wise. You could understand them perfectly as they communicated even though their mouths didn't move and they made no sounds.

The elder moon deer was wearing glasses. He and Woody Allen had a brief but meaningful exchange. And we got the permission for our picnic.

This enchanting dream of idealized nonverbal communication captures the essence of Woody Allen's uniqueness. Dream Woody's kinship with the moon deer is emphasized by his close resemblance to them. Like real-life Woody, the deer are small, intelligent, sensitive and wise. Moreover, they "don't like people very much. It's not that they're hostile; they're just very shy." The elder moon deer, presumably the wisest one of all, was even wearing glasses.

In this dream Woody Allen appears to be a link between the physical world, represented by the earth, and the spirit world, represented by the moon and moon deer. The image of a human relating to animals always suggests a spiritual connection. And lunar symbolism is often concerned with death as the first condition of mystical regeneration. The moon's periodic disappearance and subsequent reappearance represents spiritual rebirth. Since Allen is obsessed with death, the moon is a particularly appropriate setting for demonstrating his role in this dream as a link between the two worlds.

•

APRIL AUGUSTINIAK is a twenty-nine-year-old film editor who moved from Ohio to New York in 1974 in order to be near Woody Allen. April comes closer than any other dreamer to fitting the stereotype of a groupie. She has seen her idol many times in many places because her main pastime is following him around Manhattan. In fact, she's become so expert at locating the artist around town that Ron Galella, the notorious paparazzo, asked her to keep *him* posted on Allen's whereabouts. April especially loves Allen's *New Yorker* stories, and although she refuses to pick a favorite Allen movie, she concedes, "*Interiors* is way up there." She denies she's a groupie, and in one sense perhaps she's not: her goal is not to sleep with Woody but to edit his films.

April has been dreaming about Woody Allen since she was in high school. In spite of the varied sites where she's spotted the artist in waking life, most of her dreams are limited to one location, the sculpture garden of the Museum of Modern Art in Manhattan. She's had the dream below many times.

―――――――――――――― **MOMA** ――――――――――――――

It was very dark. The fountains were lit. Everything was stark. There were one thousand extras. I was watching Woody Allen shoot a film in the sculpture garden.

He looked at me and I looked back. And he maintained the eye contact. I was embarrassed, but mostly overjoyed. He looked curious. He looked interested.

Several women who've encountered real-life Allen mention his looking at them with an unflinching gaze. This contrasts with the filmmaker's manner when being introduced to someone, professionally or socially, when he is often too self-conscious to look the person in the eyes.

•

EVELYN MURPHY is a fifty-nine-year-old jazz aficionado and Mensa member who grew up in a Baptist family in Missouri. Evelyn thinks of herself as a survivor. "I had a traumatic childhood and I've long been aware of the value of laughter as healing." She thinks of Woody Allen as "a strong, strong person . . . a person who dares to be himself and who does not kowtow to the crowd and the mores of society." She says she has always been inhibited, "feeling that I should be like other people for the sake of my family, or my ex-husband, or my children. . . . I was brought up with the 'what will the neighbors say' attitude, and keeping to that meant not expressing what was in my gut, what was there wanting to be expressed." Evelyn remembers dreams only once every few months. The dream below is from 1980.

SOUL MATE

I was looking at a black-and-white collage. It was about twenty-four by thirty, and in the lower right corner was a picture of Woody Allen. His face seemed to be looking right at me, gazing at me out of the frame. As I looked more closely at the collage, I saw that it included other pictures as well. One was of a young woman with long dark hair. I thought it might be Ali McGraw, but now that I've met you [the author], I think the picture may have been of you. I began to study the collage to see if I could recognize anyone else.

The next thing I knew I was walking along a street in New York City! It was night and the whole world was in beautiful black and white.

Near a corner I stopped and looked across the street. Woody had just stepped up onto the curb. He continued striding along very purposefully. I knew he was on his way to jam.

As he strode along, Woody turned around and looked over his left shoulder. He caught my eye, and there was, for each of us, a moment of acute awareness of the other's gaze.

Although I had gone to bed feeling lonely, I woke up knowing that there was someone I could really identify with. I felt that I had found a soul mate.

Most of Evelyn's dreams are "a mishmash of Technicolor scenes in which [she is] constantly the loser." So she experienced great relief with this dream, "in beautiful black and white," wherein she finds a soul mate. The most recent Allen film Evelyn had seen before her dream was *Manhattan*, and she had marveled at its black-and-white splendor. So the black and white of her dream served to underscore the idea that this was a unique and important dream and that it was a Woody dream. The collage coming to life in Evelyn's dream is reminiscent of Stephen Wohl's dream in which the movie he was watching came to life and, like Evelyn, he was suddenly transported from L.A. into a New York City street scene complete with Woody Allen. These magical transformations also bring to mind Allen's short story, "The Kugelmass Episode," where Kugelmass, through the aid of the Great Persky and his magic cabinet, can be projected into the novel of his choice. (And, as Persky explains to the initially skeptical Kugelmass, "Not just a novel, either. A short story, a play, a poem.")

Evelyn said that her dream, which begins with her on the outside looking in and ends with her making contact with Dream Woody, reinforced her motivation to become more her own person, as well, of course, as her desire to meet Woody Allen. Her identification with Allen, sharpened in her awareness by the dream, gives her the support she is missing from her friends and family, support that pushes her to be more independent and to take risks.

Toward the end of *Manhattan*, Ike is visiting with Emily (Anne Byrne), whose husband has left her to live with the woman Ike was previously living with. "You seeing anybody?" Emily asks Ike, to which he replies: "Uh, uh, y-you-you know, I-I n-n-never had any problem meeting women." Dream Woody doesn't have any problems meeting women prefer the sister to Connie. "No, the one I hopelessly lost my heart to that day was none other than Connie's fabulous mother, Emily. Emily Chasen, fifty-five, buxom, tanned, a ravishing pioneer face with pulled-back greying hair and round, succulent curves that expressed themselves in flawless arcs like a Brancusi. . . . my mind clicked and blinked like a computer in hopes of concocting some scheme to filch more time with this overpowering and wonderful woman. If you had asked me where I expected it to lead, I really couldn't have said. I knew only as I drove through the cold, night, autumn air that somewhere Freud, Sophocles, and Eugene O'Neill were laughing."

But Mimi's sensual dream turns dark at its conclusion as she has a sudden insight into Dream Woody's character— that he's mean and immoral. Examining the dream, we find elements that presage this conclusion: the huge German limousine, for instance, while elegant, is out of place. It's a sinister, Nazilike image.

Mimi says the dream took her by surprise. However, she had the dream shortly after seeing *Stardust Memories*, in which hostile Sandy Bates is chauffeured in a huge Rolls-Royce. Mimi says the movie did not affect her opinion of Allen, though "it showed a very mean side of him. . . . I feel he's doing something I might not understand, but he's obviously doing something for reasons of his own." Ultimately, Mimi decided that "everyone is making him into this mythic figure, and I think in this dream of mine he didn't want to be . . . . I even wanted to go see the movie again, because I only saw it once and I don't think that's fair."

•

BILL MONTE is a former trumpet player who now works for Home Box Office and writes fiction. He once wrote for comedians and did stand-up comedy himself, before moving from Chicago to Los Angeles. Bill used to be obsessed with

Woody Allen, with the persona who was "an awkward person as romantic hero ... that was my fantasy of myself, too." Now Bill has come to the juncture where, he says, he needs to "overcome my mentor, as Nietzsche says. . . . You come to where you're equal with your mentor and then you have to go beyond that, and there's some sort of breaking off. . . ." For Bill, breaking off from Allen is related to the fact that "Woody's films rose in economic structure as his personal income rose. I saw *Manhattan* and, to a lesser extent, *Annie Hall*, as being about people I had no connection with whatsoever. There was an economic barrier between them and me, whereas *Bananas* and *Sleeper* were much more universal in terms of an alienated character." Bill intends to keep his work universal, even when it becomes commercially successful. The following dream, from January 8, 1979, is the first of three dreams Bill has had about Allen.

GETTING PHYSICAL

Initially I was observing the scenes in this dream before I entered them. My dream began in a very mannered, proper British room, where Woody Allen and several people I did not know were sitting on a sofa and some living room chairs, sipping tea.

The scene then shifted to a rowdy Western bar, a rough-and-tumble place with peanuts and beer. Woody was lying on top of a table watching a football game on a videobeam. A hooker in garter belts entered the room. Up close you could see she was disfigured: her eyes were out of position and she was ugly. There were a lot of men around, looking at her, but she ignored them, instead looking intently at Woody Allen. Woody didn't look at her, but the hooker noticed that even though he was watching the football game instead of her, he had an erection. The other men in the bar went over and got Woody, picked him up off the table and brought him to the hooker so she could perform fellatio on him. He protested verbally as the men brought him to her, but he didn't really resist.

Next we were out on the street in front of the bar. I was a part of the group now. A woman came running up the street. She was hysterical. She was Woody's girlfriend and she was crying about the letters he'd sent her. At this point, Woody and the hooker came out of the bar together, and Woody began telling his girlfriend off. "You just keep on!" he said. "I'm over here now and my world is a completely different place!" Then Woody and all of us walked away.

Later Woody and I and two of the others were in front of a TV monitor, watching an instant playback of what had just happened. And I said, referring to Woody's proclamation to his old girlfriend, "That is a really great moment!" And Woody replied, "Yes, it was because of that moment that I knew I had talent."

Next, the four of us lay down on a sidewalk in downtown L.A. We were waiting for two friends of Woody's, who were supposed to be private investigators. Finally we saw them coming, but they were the two men from *Waiting for Godot*. They were even carrying umbrellas while the sun was shining. And when they got to us, they kept on walking past us.

Bill says his dream has to do with Allen's separation of the physical from the mental side of life and his desire to live more in the physical world—in the world of football and sex, rather than in an intellectual's drawing room discussing *Waiting for Godot*. The dream reminded Bill of the scene from *Annie Hall* when Alvy and his wife, Robin, are at a party with magazine publishers and literary figures, and Alvy sneaks into the bedroom and turns on a Knicks game on TV. Robin discovers Alvy and asks him: "Alvy, what is so fascinating about a group of pituitary cases trying to stuff the ball through a hoop?" And Alvy replies: "What's fascinating is that it's physical. You know, it's one thing about intellectuals.

They prove that you can be absolutely brilliant and have no idea what's going on. But on the other hand ... the body doesn't lie, as—as we now know."

Allen mentions the benefits of being physical again in *Manhattan*, in a cocktail party scene in which Isaac gives his view on relating to Nazis: "W-e-e-elll, a satirical piece in the *Times* is one thing, but bricks and baseball bats really get right to the point down there." Isaac discounts the significance of intellect in yet another scene from that film, in a conversation with Mary when he says, "All right, he was a genius and Helen's a genius. You know a lot of geniuses, you know. Uh, you should meet some stupid people once in a while. You know, you could learn something." Of course, in real life, Allen has often spoken of his wish that he could have been an athlete, a wish that was briefly fulfilled for Leonard Zelig in *Zelig* as he lined up behind Babe Ruth to await his turn at bat.

Bill's dream is also, I think, about Dream Woody's move from an uptight, inhibited world to a nonrepressed one; from the proper British room to the rough-and-tumble bar and the hooker in garter belts. Bill seems to be using Dream Woody as an example for himself. He observes and weighs Dream Woody's behavior, even watching an instant playback to confirm his appraisal of Dream Woody's actions. The dichotomy between action and passivity is seen throughout the dream: Bill shifts between being an observer and being a member of the group; Dream Woody is lying on a table watching televised football; Dream Woody doesn't look at the hooker, but he still has an erection; he protests verbally (passively) but not physically to having the hooker perform fellatio on him; the four men lie passively on a sidewalk waiting for action in the form of two private investigators, who instead turn out to be the inactive characters from *Waiting for Godot*; but these characters pass them by, permitting Bill to have, perhaps, yet another chance to choose action over passivity.

The one dream scene in which Dream Woody is clearly active is when he makes his proclamation of independence from his girlfriend. "I'm over here now and my world is a completely different place!" There are three significant aspects of that move in Bill's dream. The first is that, as Dream Woody and Bill agree, it is this break with the past that confirms Dream Woody's talent. Second, the new world is not a totally appealing one: the hooker is disfigured and ugly, and even after Dream Woody's declaration of his new life, he reverts to ambivalence, lying on the sidewalk, waiting. Finally, Dream Woody's move from an inhibited world to a nonrepressed one is accomplished at the expense of hurting someone, his girlfriend. As Bill says, "I was struck in this dream by how a person can burn a bridge without any emotional caring."

•

SONIA JACOBS had dreamed, the day after her fifth wedding anniversary, about her ideal rapport with Woody Allen. In the following year, Sonia's marriage soured and her relationship with Dream Woody took a turn for the worse as well. The following dream is from November 9, 1980, a few days after Sonia separated from her husband.

BAD CONNECTION

I was staying at Woody Allen's place. And although I didn't see him often during my stay, when I did see him, I could sense something real between us.

Unfortunately the good feeling, the connection, was contradicted by my sense that Woody did not appreciate me enough.

It was clear that Woody already had everything he wanted in

life. And I was just one more accessible female trying to get his attention.

In short, Woody tried to force the connection between us with a hard on that I tried to accommodate. I was disillusioned by his using, in merely a passing, sexual way, something that could have been a wonderful connection for both of us.

Sonia's two dreams at critical points in her marriage reveal her strong desire for a total connection with someone like herself and, in the case of the second dream, her frustration at the failure of a relationship that might have had the potential to be that connection.

Sonia feels the kind of spiritual affinity for Woody Allen that she felt for her husband. This dream reveals her fear that even Woody, like her husband, would disappoint her.

•

DOREEN BENJAMIN is an editorial assistant for a magazine who finds herself believing that if she remains dissatisfied with her life she enables herself to deny the inevitability of her death. Although Doreen is a serious Allen admirer, she, like Maureen Perkins, is disturbed by his apparent elitism and womanizing. The dream below, from October 1980, gave her a chance to retaliate on the latter count.

GETTING EVEN

It was a day filled with people. It was a bright, clear day and I was strolling through New York.

As I walked along the streets, I met people—all kinds of people. And one of them was Woody Allen.

Woody and I continued to stroll through the city streets. And as we walked together we stopped and chatted with various people we encountered.

As we walked along in this casual way, Woody and I frequently lost contact with each other. The streets were teeming with people. And so, for brief periods, the two of us would be apart. Then, shortly after each parting, we would be reunited.

Each time Woody and I rejoined each other, I was aware of feeling attracted to him. And with each new meeting, I found Woody to be even more sexually appealing. Eventually I became very turned on to Woody. But, even as I was aware of my sexual desire for him, I was aware also that I would not act on that desire.

The problem was with Woody's hands: they were so pale. His hands were pale and they had freckles—freckles the same color as his hair. I knew that I could never make love with a man who had hands like that.

Woody Allen has long been letting his audiences know of his dissatisfaction with his relationships with women—of his unsuccessful attempts to find the perfect woman. He acknowledged, in an interview with Tony Schwartz for a 1980 *New York Times* article, that the longest relationship he had had with a woman in nine years (the time between his relationships with Diane Keaton and Mia Farrow) was two months. He illustrates what may be his perspective of the predicament in his story "The Lunatic's Tale":

My first wife was brilliant, but had no sense of humor. Of the Marx Brothers, she was convinced the amusing one was Zeppo. My second wife was beautiful, but lacked real passion. I recall once, while we were making love, a curious optical illusion occurred and for a split second it almost looked as though she was moving. Sharon Pflug, whom I lived with for three months, was too hostile. Whitney Weisglass was too accommodating. Pippa Mondale, a cheerful divorcée, made the fatal mistake of defending candles shaped like Laurel and Hardy.

Several of the women interviewed for this book expressed annoyance at Allen's exclusive casting of gorgeous women in his films. This charge, of course, could be directed at the majority of filmmakers, but Allen's fans expect more of him than they do of other filmmakers. Nevertheless, Allen's infatuation with physical beauty in women can hardly be denied. He actually seems to chide himself for it when the character Isaac confronts his lesbian ex-wife in *Manhattan* and she reminds him: "Well, you knew my history when you married me," to which Isaac replies: "Yeah, I know, my analyst warned me, but you were so beautiful that I—that I got another analyst." Overall, however, the women in Woody Allen's films are also intelligent, independent, likable women with their own careers and their own ideas, and they usually grow emotionally in the course of the film.

Carola Dibbell wrote in *The Village Voice* in 1979: "I take it that Woody Allen has never been big on post-'50s politics, including feminism, but he's a decent, thoughtful man, and he seems to love women." Dibbell's assessment summarizes the opinions of the majority of the women interviewed for this book and the predominant sentiments of their dreams. To classify the inner world Woody Allen projects in his work as sexist or anti-Semitic would ring unmistakably false. Still, it may be a valid grievance, expressed by several dreamers, that Allen does less than he could to contradict the image of prejudice in his films.

Why does Woody treat his woman badly in this dream? Manny says the beating scene from his dream reflects thoughts he's had in his waking life about *Manhattan*. He enjoyed the movie but subsequently read an article claiming Allen treated the women in the film badly. Looking back on the movie, he decided he agreed with the writer.

•

MAUREEN PERKINS is a thirty-one-year-old actress who has worked as an extra in two of Allen's films. She thinks Allen is a conscientious but sexist filmmaker. When Maureen was six years old she stormed around the house for days after finding out that women didn't get the right to vote until 1920, and she's recently begun writing screenplays in order to create stronger roles for women. Oddly enough, Maureen's favorite Woody Allen film is *Everything You Always Wanted to Know About Sex*, which she thinks is excellent satire.

————————— **WOODY LEARNS** —————————

It was a dazzling bright summer day, like a day on the Italian Riviera. I was sitting on one of the red stools at a counter of a Chock Full o' Nuts. Three other women sat on my side of the counter.

The other women and I were all looking across the counter. Opposite us sat Woody Allen.

I made a clever comment, an intelligent, witty remark. Woody and I looked at each other, and there was an instant recognition of a truth for each of us.

"This," I thought, "is the first time Allen's ever realized that a woman can be as funny as a man."

I felt a little relief. "Now I know why he does what he does."

The relief Maureen experienced in her dream left her hopeful that real-life Allen might see the light and become less sexist. Her dream illustrates a confrontation between women and the filmmaker, a moment of reckoning in which the women, with Maureen as their spokesperson, triumph in getting Dream Woody to see them as they see themselves. It is significant that Dream Woody accepts this revelation without a protest, indicating that the conflict was a matter of his misunderstanding, rather than one of a difference in values.

But whose misunderstanding is it in waking life? Real-life Allen seems to be drawn toward wit as well as wisdom in women. In the 1979 interview with Natalie Gittelson for *The New York Times Magazine,* Allen said of Louise Lasser (who acted with him in *Bananas*) and Diane Keaton (after her roles in *Sleeper* and *Love and Death*), "They're two huge talents— unique stylists in the entertainment world. . . . Both of them are hilariously funny. Both of them are highly, *highly* perceptive."

•

MIMI JEROME, the harpist who had dreamed earlier of a quiet first date with Dream Woody, had a second dream date with him in November 1980.

——————— **SHOCK OF RECOGNITION** ———————

It was nightfall and I was admiring Woody Allen's house on the beach. Woody had drawn the curtains for the night and opened the doors to let in the night air.

Later that night, Woody, my mother, my two sisters and I left for a concert in which I was to play. We rode in a huge German convertible limousine. On the way we drove into an elegant restaurant.

Other people were sitting at tables but Woody, my family and I were in this elegant car. I turned to Woody.

"You must feel more at home in this milieu than I do," I said.

At this moment the waiter arrived at our car with trays of pastries. There was an individual tray for each of us, and each tray contained ten different kinds of pastries!

As I surveyed my tray, I thought, "My God, I could never eat all of these." But just as I was thinking this Woody, unembarrassed, said, "Can I take your fudge one?"

"Sure," I said.

As I sat there eating my nine pastries (Woody with eleven), I noticed how Woody interacted with my mother and my two sisters. I could see that Woody's relationship with my mother was much more flowing than his relationship with me. Then I thought that Woody also liked each of my sisters better than me—Jillie, because she is so beautiful, and Annmerle, because she is extraordinarily sexy.

Even later that same night we all went to a lawn party. Woody had been ignoring me earlier in the evening, but here he started paying attention to me. In fact, Woody singled me out.

"Would you like to play volleyball or baseball?" he asked me.

"I like soccer, but I don't play lacrosse," I answered him.

I was excited because this was the first time Woody had spoken directly to me about something truly personal. I looked at his face now—*really* looked at it—for the first time. And I was startled because this real person was not like the movie figure. His very face was different.

Woody went off to eat another dinner, and I went into the bathroom to take off my long underwear. It was summer, I was hot with this long underwear on, and I suddenly realized that there was no good reason that I had to wear it!

I took off my long underwear and rearranged my hair. I tried to look older, sexier. I pinned my hair up and then I took it down. I tried several different styles. Finally, I decided it looked best down. I came out of the bathroom and looked around for Woody. I wanted to see if he had finished eating and was ready to play ball. When I couldn't find him, I walked out by the water and headed along the beach, back toward Woody's house.

I was delighted with the ocean. Along the way I jumped up and down on the shore and ran in and out of the water. Sometimes I would run in too far and a wave would come up and splash my dress.

I came across Woody on my way to his house. He was in a luncheonette on the boardwalk having dessert.

"Woody!" I called. All of the people in line turned around and stared.

"What did they feed you for dinner! Why are you eating again?" I exclaimed.

As I looked at Woody, I remembered how he had looked to me earlier in the night when he had first spoken personally to me, inviting me to play baseball or volleyball. And I thought: "This is a mean man!"

"This man," I thought, "is meaner and tougher than people think he is. And immoral, too."

For the most part, Mimi's dream is playful and sensual, even hedonistic. The lavish arrays of pastries and Dream Woody's overindulgence, Mimi's carefree splashing in the ocean waves, Dream Woody's beach house with its doors invitingly open and its windows curtained for privacy, the invitations to ball games, the lovely women and Mimi's provocative decision to remove her inappropriate long underwear and rearrange her hair, all suggest a pleasure-filled day and the frolicking spirit of *A Midsummer Night's Sex Comedy* (which came after Mimi's dream).

Mimi's jealousy of her two sisters and mother recalls Allen's short story "Retribution," in which twenty-four-year-old Harold Cohen's girlfriend, Connie ("Tall, blond, high cheekboned, an actress, a scholar, a charmer, irrevocably alienated, with a hostile and perceptive wit only challenged in its power to attract by the lewd, humid eroticism her every curve suggested") fears that Harold will prefer her younger sister. When they meet at a family gathering, Harold does *not*

Chapter 17

"OLD SOLDIERS NEVER DIE..."

GENERAL MACARTHUR left Japan on April sixteenth. Before he strode from the American Embassy for the last time, Emperor Hirohito came to say good-by. The Emperor wept openly as he expressed his nation's gratitude toward MacArthur. Later along the route to the Haneda Airport, a million Japanese turned out to wave farewell to the former Supreme Commander.

It was MacArthur's hope that he could slip back into the United States without fanfare. Little did he realize as he stepped aboard the *Bataan* the affection with which he would be treated. At Honolulu, 200,000 came out to cheer him. When he set foot on the mainland's soil at San Francisco, a crowd of 500,000 persons were waiting to pay him homage. He put an arm around his thirteen-year-old son Arthur, who had spent all his life overseas, and said, "Well, Arthur, here we are home at last."

Instead of letting him slip back silently into plain citizenry, Congress insisted that he address a Joint Session of both Houses on April 19. There was agreement that his eloquence matched that of any person who had ever addressed Congress.

He spoke with tears in his eyes, but his voice was strong. Thirty-five times his speech was interrupted by applause.

"I stand on this rostrum," MacArthur began, "with a sense of deep humility and great pride—humility in the wake of those great American architects of our history who have stood here before me, pride in the reflection that this forum of legislative debate represents human liberty in the purest form yet devised. Here are centered the hopes and aspirations and faith of the entire human race. . . .

"I trust, therefore, that you will do me the justice of receiving that which I have to say as solely expressing the considered viewpoint of a fellow American. I address you with neither rancor nor bitterness in the fading twilight of life with but one purpose in mind: to serve my country."

He spoke of the war and pointed out that "the Communist threat is a global one. . . . You cannot appease or otherwise surrender to communism in Asia without simultaneously undermining our efforts to halt its advance in Europe." He pointed out that in Asia were "half of the earth's population and 60 per cent of its natural resources." He told Congress that what these people long under the heel of colonialism wanted from the United States was "friendly guidance, understanding and support, not imperialist direction; the dignity of equality and not the shame of subjugation."

He went into the situation in various countries of Asia. On the Korean conflict, which led to his release from command, he said, "While I was not consulted prior to the President's decision to intervene in support of the Republic of Korea, that decision, from a military standpoint, proved a sound one. As I say, it proved a sound one, as we hurled back the invader and decimated his forces. Our victory was complete and our objectives within reach when Red China intervened with numerically superior ground forces.

"This created a new war and an entirely new situation, a situation not contemplated when our forces were committed against the North Korean invaders, a situation which called for new decisions in the diplomatic sphere to permit the realistic adjustment of military strategy.

"Such decisions have not been forthcoming. . . . We could hold in Korea by constant maneuver . . . but we could hope at best for only an indecisive campaign with its terrible and constant attrition upon our forces."

As for his wish to blockade China and to send planes north of the Yalu, he said, "Efforts have been made to distort my position. It has been said in effect that I was a warmonger. Nothing could be further from the truth. I know war as few other men now living know it, and nothing, to me, is more revolting. . . . But once war is forced upon us, there is no alternative than to apply every available means to bring it to a swift end. War's very objective is victory, not prolonged indecision."

His finishing remarks brought tears to many of his listeners. "I am closing my fifty-two years of military service. When I joined the Army, even before the turn of the century, it was the fulfillment of all my boyish hopes and dreams.

"The world has turned over many times since I took the oath on the plain at West Point, and the hopes and dreams have long since vanished. But I still remember the refrain of one of the most popular barracks ballads of that day, which proclaimed, most proudly, that 'Old soldiers never die. They just fade away.'

"And like the old soldier of that ballad, I now close my military career and just fade away—an old soldier who tried to do his duty as God gave him the light to see that duty. Good-by."

MacArthur did not fade away. When he went to New York to establish a home for himself and his family at the Waldorf-Astoria, police estimated that a crowd of 7,500,000 saw him nod greetings in his old trench coat and battered, gold-braided military cap as he rode from La Guardia Airport to the hotel.

A short time later a Joint Senate Committee on Armed Services and Foreign Relations invited him to testify on the military situation in the Far East and on his release from duty. He answered questions for three straight days. Afterward the Committee praised him for his "physical endurance, the vastness of your patience and the thoughtfulness and frankness with which you have answered all questions drawing freely on your vast reservoir of knowledge and experience."

MacArthur could not sit idly by. Only a few months after his return he went on a speaking tour that carried him to eleven states. He called it a crusade to awaken the people both to domestic and foreign policy. He continued to criticize the "passive defense" military policy in Korea.

In the spring of 1952, several of MacArthur's friends asked him to run for President on the Republican ticket. Although he would not permit them to promote his cause, he did agree to deliver the keynote address before the Republican National Convention that July. When he strode onto the convention floor and to the platform, he was greeted with a wild ovation. During his speech delegates treated him to interruptions of prolonged applause. Afterward, former President Herbert Hoover and others begged him to remain at the convention so they could help him win the nomination. However, he refused and caught the first commercial flight back to New York.

It was after that convention that MacArthur began a new career. At the age of seventy-two, he hung up his uniform and gold-braided cap, donned civilian clothes and went to work. When the Sperry Corporation combined with Remington Rand, MacArthur was elected chairman of the board of the new Sperry Rand.

He continued to take a special interest in the Korean conflict, which did not end until July, 1953, when both sides agreed to a truce. The battered country was once more divided almost as it had been before the fighting started. More than two years before, on March 24, 1951, after the Pentagon had refused him permission to bomb beyond the Yalu, MacArthur had offered a similar cease-fire truce to the Chinese Red commander in Korea. For making his proposal, he had been officially scolded by the Joint Chiefs of Staff. There was, of course, no way of knowing whether the Chinese Reds would have agreed to a truce at that time. In the two-year "accordion war" that went on after MacArthur left Korea, American casualties totaled 80,000. This was higher than those suffered under MacArthur's command during the savage battles up and down the length of the country.

The years began slipping past. Busy with his job, and delivering eloquent speeches which grew more infrequent as time went on, MacArthur celebrated his eightieth birthday in January, 1960. In March of that year, he underwent a serious operation but recovered completely.

On June 21, 1960, Japan awarded him the highest decoration it could confer on a foreigner who was not a head of state. This was the Insignia of the Grand Cordon of the

Order of the Rising Sun with Paulownia Flowers. Emperor Hirohito also sent him a signed scroll.

Said General MacArthur: "No honor I have ever received moves me more deeply. Perhaps this is because I can recall no parallel in history where a great nation recently at war has so distinguished its former enemy commander."

MacArthur's hair has become thin. But his back is still straight and he holds his head high. He continues to stride like a cadet on dress parade.

From a lifetime that reads like a unique adventure novel, he has emerged in his nation's history as one of its most valorous and able defenders. A hero and a military genius he will always be.

To future generations he points to the motto of West Point as a standard to live by. It served him well and will no doubt inspire others. It should be his epitaph—"Duty, honor and country."

SELECTED BIBLIOGRAPHY

Considine, Robert B., *MacArthur the Magnificent*. David McKay Co., Inc., 1942

Gunther, John, *Riddle of MacArthur*. Harper and Brothers, 1951

Hunt, Frazier, *MacArthur and the War Against Japan*. Charles Scribner's Sons, 1944

————, *Untold Story of Douglas MacArthur*. The Devin-Adair Co., 1954

Kelley, Frank R., *MacArthur*. Doubleday and Company, Inc., 1950

Kenney, George C., *The MacArthur I Knew*. Duell, Sloan and Pearce, Inc., 1951

Lee, Clark G. and Henschel, Richard, *Douglas MacArthur*. Henry Holt and Co., Inc., 1952

MacArthur, Douglas, *Address at a Joint Meeting of the Two Houses in the Hall of the House of Representatives*. 1951

Miller, Francis T., *General Douglas MacArthur*. The John C. Winston Co., 1942

Rovere, Richard and Schlesinger, Arthur, Jr., *The General and the President*. Farrar, Straus, 1952

Spanier, J. W., *The Truman-MacArthur Controversy*. Belknap Press of Harvard University Press, 1959

Whitney, Courtney, *MacArthur: His Rendezvous With History*. Alfred A. Knopf, Inc., 1955

Willoughby, Charles A., *MacArthur: 1941-1951*. McGraw-Hill Book Co., Inc., 1956

INDEX